# TEN
# *Somerset*
# MYSTERIES

## TRUE TALES
## FROM THE COUNTY

## Charles Whynne-Hammond

COUNTRYSIDE BOOKS
NEWBURY, BERKSHIRE

First Published 1995
© Charles Whynne-Hammond 1995

COUNTRYSIDE BOOKS
3 Catherine Road
Newbury, Berkshire

ISBN 1 85306 359 2

Designed by Mon Mohan
Line illustrations by Glenys Jones

Produced through MRM Associates Ltd., Reading
Typeset by Paragon Typesetters, Queensferry, Clwyd
Printed by J. W. Arrowsmith Ltd., Bristol

# CONTENTS

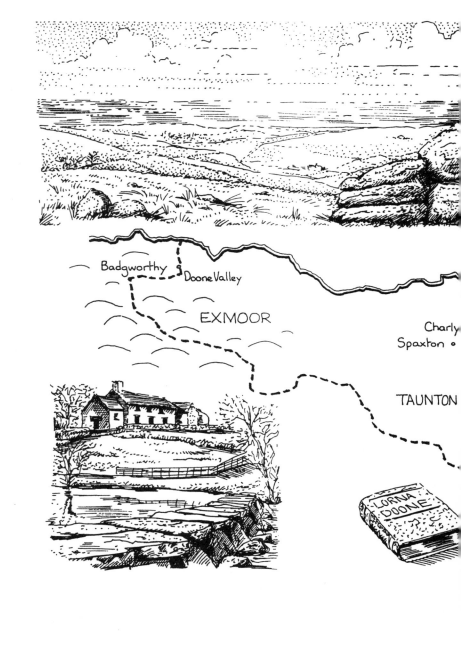

Badgworthy

Doone Valley

EXMOOR

Charly

Spaxton o

TAUNTON

LORNA DOONE

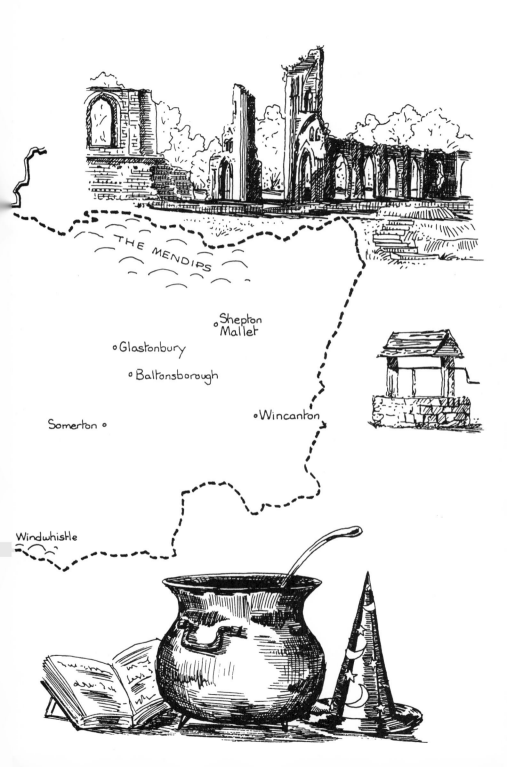

THE MENDIPS

Shepton Mallet

Glastonbury

Baltonsborough

Somerton

Wincanton

Windwhistle

# ACKNOWLEDGEMENTS

I should like to thank all those who helped in my research: David Bromwich and Liz Clark at the Local History Library in Taunton and the various friends, neighbours and villagers of Somerset who have supplied important information. I should also like to thank Glenys Jones for her attractive and evocative sketches, my brother Alex for his invaluable suggestions and Gwen Cassell for helping with the final draft.

Charles Whynne-Hammond
Autumn 1995

# 1

# THE SENSUAL STONES

The mystery of the ancient
summer dwellers' ley lines

From the top of Burrow Mump, just eight miles north-east of Taunton, you can look across the broad, green, watery meadows of the Somerset Levels. The view is beautiful. The Mendip Hills, the Wiltshire Downs, the Dorset uplands, the Blackdowns and the Quantocks all form a blue, distant skyline, as you circle your gaze clockwise. The withy-banked rhynes – the drainage channels lined with willow trees – spread out below, across a landscape of pasture and heath. But see! One particular feature of the prospect may strike you as interesting. Look down at Othery church and notice that Glastonbury Tor rises up directly behind it. Turn round, in exactly the opposite direction, and look across to the church at Creech St Michael, close to the outskirts of Taunton. All three places, and Burrow Mump as well, are aligned, in roughly a south-west to north-east direction. Now look northwards. The church at Westonzoyland is directly in line with the more distant church at Bawdrip. Such lines in the landscape may not be coincidental. Some people say they are ley lines, and as such are almost as old as history itself.

The Somerset Levels may be seen as the cradle of civilisation in Britain. During the Iron Age – and indeed in earlier periods too – Glastonbury was a focal point for human activity. There was a pagan shrine here, and a military fortification. A trading settlement was located here also and early man built tracks across the Levels to link up separate farming villages. The Levels were much wetter than they are today and boats could sail up the rivers to the harbours that were scattered along the edge of the surrounding uplands. Towns and villages like Bridgwater, Taunton, Langport and Dundon began life as Celtic ports, trading with places as far afield as Europe and the eastern Mediterranean.

Somerset in those days was a thriving farming area. In the winter months cattle and sheep were kept in the hills that rise saucer-like around the perimeter of the marshy Levels, but in the summer months, when the fens dried out, farmers would bring their animals down to the watery meadows for rich grazing. These meadows, in consequence, became known as the 'summer lands' and the farmers were called the 'summer dwellers'. And it was these dwellers – the summer settlers – that later gave the present county its name.

Ley lines probably date back to the days when these summer dwellers were amongst the wealthiest and most advanced peoples in Britain. There are ley lines to be found everywhere, but they seem to have a particular concentration in this part of the West Country. Some of the largest and most famous ley lines of all, like the St Michael Line, run through the heart of the Somerset Levels, and numerous smaller and less well-known ones criss-cross the area with unerring regularity.

So, what exactly are ley lines? How were they discovered and when did they evolve? And why are so many of them to be found in this strange landscape of fen and heath? Is it that these ancient summer dwellers actually developed the ley lines themselves, or did they merely harness a feature already in existence?

Back in 1920 a certain Alfred Watkins was riding across his native county of Herefordshire. Atop one hill he pulled up his horse to admire the view. The Welsh Marches lay below him, shimmering in the sunshine. But then he experienced a strange revelation. Across the landscape, and superimposed upon the fields, hedges, farmsteads and villages, he saw a network of lines which, as he wrote later, stood out 'like glowing wires all over the surface of the country, intersecting at the sites of churches, old stones and other spots of traditional sanctity.'

6

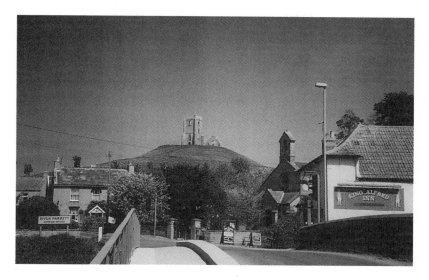

*St Michael's chapel atop Burrow Mump.*

Subsequently, Watkins studied other parts of the country and tested his theory of straight lines. As a result of this research he published a book in 1925 called *The Old Straight Track*. In this he called his alignments 'leys' because to him the word 'ley' or 'lay' had historic and philologic associations. In Saxon times it meant 'pasture', 'enclosed field' or 'forest clearing' but these meanings probably derived from an earlier definition of 'cleared track through a wood' or 'woodland glade'. In this guise the word 'ley' might have been taken from the Celtic tongue in which it is thought to have meant 'straight alignment'. Some philologists think it is from this earlier form that we still have the word 'lay' as used in such phrases as 'to lay a gun' (to aim a gun) and a 'batten lay' (a batten in a loom, used for straightening thread).

Watkins believed these ley lines were merely trackways, linking sites of antiquity. Just as the Romans did in later centuries, so Neolithic or Bronze Age people created routes across the country using the easiest method of surveying. By identifying natural landscape features, summits or beacons, the early surveyors would draw straight routes between

7

places and then put down marker points between each hilltop. These markers might be mounds, upright stones, earth cuttings, clumps of trees or excavated 'notches' in the topography. In time, Watkins argued, these straight tracks became major routeways and developed their own staging posts. Where they crossed rivers, major bridging-points evolved, and where they crossed each other, settlements would appear. Stone circles, moated islands, hillforts and various pagan shrines were also built along these leys, and wells or ponds were dug to provide water for thirsty travellers. Since many pagan sites were transformed by the first Christians into holy places, so churches frequently appeared upon ley lines. Almost every church discovered to be on a ley line is said to be founded upon an ancient pagan shrine. The same is true of castles, moot halls, monasteries and chapels. Invariably such buildings, when found on ley lines, are situated on ancient sites. In Saxon and medieval times architects and builders normally used features already in existence – a Norman castle would be placed on a Celtic mound for example, a moot hall at a spot long used for tribal meetings.

Thus, according to Watkins, when the Romans arrived in Britain, they found a country already crossed by a network of planned, straight tracks. On top of this they merely added their own network of straight roads, these mostly radiating out from London (then called Londinium). Where the Romans found that a section of their own alignment joined an earlier one, they simply widened and paved the existing length of routeway. In this way, it has been found, many ley lines are followed by Roman roads.

Since *The Old Straight Track* was published, much more research has been done into ley lines. For a start, it was soon discovered that straight alignments are not only found in England. They are to be seen all over the world and can be dated to the dawn of time. Across the savanna lands of southern Africa, over the deserts of the Middle East and – most remarkably – in the Andes of Peru and Mexico, there are long, straight markings to be seen in the landscape. Those in South America continue for hundreds of miles and are scratched into the mountain rocks. Seen from the air they are spectacular indeed. The native Indians call them siqi, 'lines of things', and around the old Inca capital of Cuzco they radiate out in all directions.

At the time, Alfred Watkins' theory was dismissed by many historians and geographers, who said that early man was insufficiently 'developed' to construct a sophisticated route network. But, as our knowledge of the Neolithic period, Bronze Age and Celtic times expands, so people are beginning to reappraise the whole question of ley lines. In fact, an entire field of study has opened up, with enthusiasts corroborating and enlarging Watkins' original findings. Numerous books have been published specifically on the subject of ley lines and there is even a regular monthly magazine, called *The Ley Hunter*.

But the more that is learnt about ley lines, the more is Watkins' initial reasoning being questioned. Yes, say many experts, ley lines do exist but, no, they were not constructed as trackways. What lies behind ley lines, these experts now say, is far more complex than Watkins believed. They could be linked, instead, to astronomical patterns, being aligned with the stars in the heavens. Or else they could be associated with the latent energy held within the earth's crust.

From certain studies of ley lines in general, and of those in Somerset in particular, it appears that these alignments have an ethereal quality. Stones found along their routes give off a sensual energy. People claiming to possess hypersensitive powers of emotion say that, by touching these ley-line stones, they receive a physical sensation, sometimes little more than a tingle, sometimes a violent shock like an electric discharge. If this is true, what powers lie hidden within these ley lines? What subtle energy lies within their ancient stones?

The famous St Michael Ley Line was first identified by John Michell during the 1960s, and was further studied by Hamish Miller and Paul Broadhurst in the 1970s. It runs across the entire breadth of southern England from St Michael's Mount, off the coast of west Cornwall, to Bury St Edmunds and the East Anglian coast – a total length of more than 300 miles. Along its route it passes through some of the

*Glastonbury Tor – the centre of at least five ley lines.*

largest and best known archaeological sites in Britain, including Brentor, Glastonbury Tor and Avebury. Here in Somerset it enters the county from the south-west over the Blackdown Hills and runs through St Michael's church, Trull (south of Taunton). From there it passes through the church at Creech St Michael, Burrow Mump, Othery church and Glastonbury Tor, before reaching Stoke St Michael church in the Mendips and the church at Woolverton near Rode. Further north-east it crosses the county boundary into Wiltshire to reach Avebury.

All along this route are megalithic monuments and various other prehistoric sites, some of which are small and half-forgotten. Perhaps the most significant fact of all about the alignment of the St Michael Line is that it exactly coincides with the direction of the rising sun on the old May Day, a date of great importance in the ancient, pagan calendar. Early man knew exact details about the solar cycle and held festivals at certain times according to the position of the sun. The midsummer solstice has much to do with the layout of Stonehenge, it is believed, and this gives further evidence to

10

the theory that past civilisations were more astronomically aware than was once supposed.

Whereas Michell, in his original study of the St Michael Line, assumed the route ran straight, Miller and Broadhurst researched the alignment from a different perspective. They looked at ways in which the various stones along the route gave off different levels of seismic energy. Using numerous methods of exploration, including highly scientific measuring instruments that registered subtle changes in electro-energy, they discovered that other mysterious lines co-existed. These were serpentine in nature, flowing along in the same general direction as the St Michael Line but weaving in and out in a series of curves. Two lines in particular were discovered, which Miller and Broadhurst named the Michael Line and Mary Line. Since then expert dowsers and water diviners have further studied these two lines and they have confirmed that they do exist.

What became especially fascinating was the fact that the Michael and Mary Lines were found to link many more ancient sites than did the simple St Michael ley line. At each of these sites, it was also discovered, the energy recorded by ultrasonic detectors appeared to rise sharply. Especially high vibrations were measured at such stone monuments as the remains of the old church at Burrow Bridge, the tower that tops Glastonbury Tor (St Michael's Tower) and the megaliths known as the Devil's Bed and Bolster, near Rode – each site being on or alongside the St Michael ley. It was as though these Michael and Mary Lines were lines of energy which harnessed the forces from within the earth. Such ancient sites as stone circles and standing stones seemed to produce 'pulses'. If this were true then it appeared that, across the country as a whole, ley lines were actually force lines which created a kind of National Grid of enhanceable energy. But unlike our modern National Grid, along which power is lost, this prehistoric grid gained strength with length as each stone site it passed through became a 'booster station'. Perhaps ancient tribes – far from being primitive – were highly advanced in particular skills. They understood the complex forces under the landscape and knew how to harness them.

*The market cross at Somerton — a focal point for radiating ley lines.*

The town of Somerton stands in the heart of the Somerset Levels and is at the centre of a radiating network of ley lines. It is in the middle of an 'island' of hills that rise up between the rivers Yeo and Cary. Once a focal point for the summer dwellers, it later became an important market town and, indeed, a major administrative centre, being the original 'capital' of Somerset.

Three of the lines that run through the town may be described here, for they are clear and can easily be traced out on a map. The first was identified by Rosemary Clinch in 1990 and runs roughly north to south. Northwards from Somerton it leads directly to Castle Hill, possible site of a hill-fort, and then to New Ditch, an ancient earthwork standing in Butleigh Wood, crossing an old Roman site on the way. Beyond, it runs to Glastonbury Tor and then via numerous cairns and burrows to Priddy, up on the Mendips. Priddy is an ancient site indeed, with any number of antiquities scattered on the hillside. Southwards from Somerton the ley line runs to the knoll at Knole, near Long Sutton, and then down to the churches at Stoke sub

12

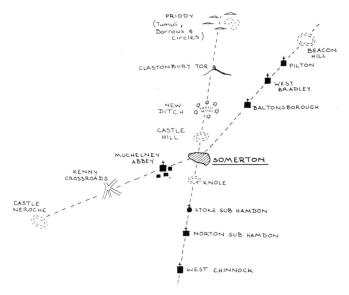

*The Somerton leys.*

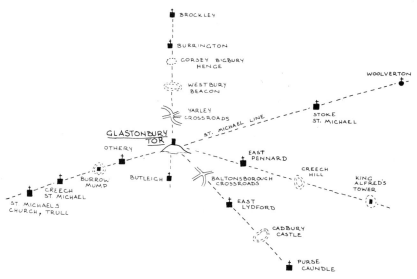

*The Glastonbury leys.*

13

Hamdon, Norton sub Hamdon and West Chinnock.

The second ley line from Somerton runs south-westwards. This passes through Muchelney (where stands the medieval monastery whose church and some abbey ruins still survive) and goes on to Castle Neroche, site of a Celtic hillfort on the Blackdown Hills, which later became the motte of a Norman castle. On its way this ley line also runs through the old crossroads at Kenny, near Ashill, and over Barrington Hill, thought to have been the site of an old beacon.

The third ley line from Somerton runs north-eastwards, eventually reaching Beacon Hill on the Mendip Hills near Oakhill, where there are numerous tumuli. On its way this alignment passes through no fewer than three churches, those at Baltonsborough, West Bradley and Pilton. All these churches have been built over or close to sites of pagan shrines.

There are several other ley lines leading from Somerton but these still require further investigation. One of these is thought to link Ilchester, on the Foss Way, to Summer House Hill, Yeovil. Another may run eastward to Ballands Castle, near Penselwood, via Charlton Adam and North Barrow. No doubt there are more ley lines still to be discovered.

Further north, Glastonbury is also the centre for a network of radiating ley lines, and must be one of the most important sites in Europe for its links with the ancient world. There are profound mysteries here and the town is heavy with strange happenings. Superstition and legend commingle and the air is full of mystic energy. There is the story of King Arthur and Avalon, and the tale of the coming of the infant Jesus, who travelled to Britain with his uncle, Joseph of Arimathea. The Holy Grail is said to lie hidden hereabouts and the Holy Thorn continues to blossom each year at Christmas. On the top of the Tor, where the ruined tower of St Michael stands sentinel, people tell of strange occurrences – dramatic weather conditions, supernatural experiences and odd psychic sensations. A few hypersensitive visitors have even felt a power oozing out from the scattered stones, electric-like currents surging up from the rocky depths.

One of the longest ley lines passing through Glastonbury

Tor – except for the St Michael Line itself – is the one that runs for some 20 miles from Brockley church in the north (beyond the Mendips) to Butleigh church in the south. Between Glastonbury and Brockley this ley line passes through the Yarley crossroads (site of an ancient market stone), Westbury Beacon (site of a hillfort), Gorsey Bigbury (where there is a Neolithic henge) and Burrington village (where the church stands on a pagan shrine).

Another ley line runs eastward from the Tor to King Alfred's Tower, on the Somerset-Wiltshire border. King Alfred's Tower stands on Kings Settle Hill, a few miles north of Wincanton. The tower itself was built in the 18th century to commemorate the Saxon victory over the Danes in AD 879, but the site is much more historic. This hilltop is thought to have been a meeting place for tribes during pre-Christian times. It was here that boundary disputes were settled. Significantly, the place still stands close to a three-county border, for Somerset, Wiltshire and Dorset all join nearby. This importance as a Bronze Age or Celtic meeting place continued through Saxon times and Alfred is said to have raised his standard here before his battle with the invading Vikings. Between Glastonbury Tor and King Alfred's Tower the ley line passes through the church at East Pennard and the top of Creech Hill, site of an Iron Age hill-fort.

A longer ley line than this one stretches from Glastonbury Tor south-eastwards into Dorset. This takes in the ancient sites of Cadbury Castle (fabled site of King Arthur's Camelot) and Purse Caundle where stands a church built on a pagan temple. Between the Tor and Cadbury Castle the line also cuts across the long-standing crossroads at Baltonsborough (the village where St Dunstan was born) and East Lydford, a hamlet standing close to the bridging-point where the Roman Foss Way crossed the river Brue.

So three clear ley lines run through Glastonbury Tor, in addition to the famous St Michael Line. Others are probably still to be found. It is hard to imagine that all these alignments are purely coincidental.

Ancient peoples – those who farmed, mined and traded, those who lived close to nature and knew its secrets – were not savages. When the ancient civilisations of Mesopotamia, China, Egypt and Greece were flourishing, the tribes living in Britain were not barbaric, as historians used to think. They too had intelligence, skills and culture. But these attributes were not of the conventional kind. They were born out of a deep knowledge of the landscape, and of the universe, around them. The early settlers of Somerset, the summer dwellers, knew intimately the world into which they had been created.

Increasingly, archaeologists are beginning to understand that our ancient sites could have been built for a deliberate intent and with specific qualities. Just as the pyramids in Egypt are thought to have been constructed in accordance with the patterns of the planets, the constellations and the Milky Way, so too may the stone monuments of Britain have been erected according to the laws of the universe. Those prehistoric builders had a fundamental grasp of mathematics and geometry – they could survey accurately and they could forecast the heavenly movements. The sun was the giver of life and was worshipped accordingly. It seems only natural that some of the alignments created on the earth should have related to the sun's varied movements across the sky. Long ley lines could have been oriented to the sun or moon, shorter ley lines could have been oriented to other planets or to the distant stars.

Might this be less than the whole story, however? A few people hold that leys are orthotenic lines – that is, lines of magnetic current. As such they could have been constructed to help the navigation of UFOs, the hillforts and stone circles sited along their routes acting as landmarks. Other people, perhaps more realistically, offer another explanation, that ley lines focus the forces of 'serpent energy'.

Those ley lines that curve, serpent-like, such as the Michael and Mary Lines that cross the Somerset Levels, may in fact channel the earth's spirit. A divine force, in other words, is concentrated along particular alignments, and sensual stones enable that force to be harnessed. Certainly, it is known that serpent energy was a concept adopted by the Druids, in which serpents or dragons were used as symbolic images for the power of nature. Nor were the Druids alone in this idea. The aboriginal tribes of Australia use wandering 'dream paths' to honour the spirit of the land, and the dragon remains a potent symbol in the Far East. In ancient Egypt there was Ureaus, a cobra-like serpent that coiled around the heads of gods and pharaohs, and in ancient Greece Hermes the god of healing had a serpent staff.

Traditional British folklore revolves around the dragon, the serpentine creature that was the visible sign of nature's power. The Celts worshipped dragons, and hilltops were sacred because they were the places where dragons lived. When the Christian missionaries arrived they adopted and adapted this symbol. They built churches on hilltops and dedicated them to St Michael, the slayer of dragons. Perhaps it is no coincidence that the St Michael Line is so named. And perhaps it is no coincidence that so many hilltop churches in and around the Somerset Levels are dedicated to the same St Michael.

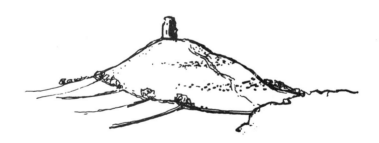

# 2

# THE HEALING WATERS
# OF MENDIP

The mystery of the powers of springs
and wells from time immemorial

All over the Mendip Hills, and around the upland fringes,
there are wells and springs that are said to possess mysterious
powers. What are these powers? Do they really exist or are
they just make-believe? Legend says they can bring good
health, can cure physical ailments or can relieve mental
anguish. It is said they are holy and bring forth goodness. But
why? And how? Or are these wells and springs merely the
leftovers of an age when people were ignorant and
superstitious, when people believed anything that might
make their lives less miserable?

At Witham Friary, south of Frome, there is St Dunstan's
Well whose water was reputed to have cured epilepsy. Puck's
Well, at Rode, which is north of Frome, and Bully Well at
Chew Magna, which is south-west of Keynsham, were both
said to have cured eye complaints. St Anne's Well in Bristol
was once so famous for its health-giving properties that
Henry VII himself went there with his queen. At Pilton there
were two wells, both sanctified for their medicinal qualities
and much visited in the Middle Ages by pilgrims on their way
to Glastonbury. Originally of greater fame were St Julian's
Well at Wellow, north-east of Radstock, and the waters at
Doulting, east of Shepton Mallet. The former traditionally
brought good fortune and longevity, the latter gave relief
from nervous disorders. Can these places really have grown
up purely out of superstition? Or might there really have
been something about the water that poured forth from

the ground at those places?

And then there is Bath, of course. The hot springs there have been used since pre-Christian times to aid human recovery from illness. It would be hard to believe the waters at Bath do not possess special qualities. And if these do, why not other waters that flow out from the Mendip rocks?

The story is told of how Bladud, son of the legendary Lud Hudibras, eighth king of the Britons, first discovered the healing springs of Bath. It is an ancient story and much repeated, but no one knows how true it is. As with many legends there is probably an element of veracity.

In about the year 863 BC Prince Bladud, grandson of King Lear, the monarch who inspired one of Shakespeare's plays, contracted leprosy. He was thus banished from the royal court. But his mother, full of pity, gave him a ring as a keepsake and told him that, should he ever be cured, he could return. He left and became a travelling swineherd, getting work where best he could, sleeping rough and living off the bounty of the hedgerows. He travelled far, and wandered over the Cotswolds.

One day the pigs he was tending became afflicted with his disease and grew ill. Afraid that their owner would find out, he drove them across the river Avon, away from the farmer's land. The spot where they crossed is still called Swineford. Upon the far side of the river the pigs rooted for acorns and Bladud worried about his future. He was sorely troubled. The Avon valley was wooded and marshy, the Mendip Hills to the south were barren and windswept. He wondered where he could go and what he could do with his diseased pigs.

Then a strange thing happened. Panicking at a sudden sound, the pigs rushed up the valley and plunged accidentally into a black, foul-smelling bog where various small springs issued forth. With difficulty Bladud waded in after them and hauled the animals out. And lo! He found the pigs were no longer leprous. Looking at his own body he saw too that his arms and legs, which had been immersed in the muddy waters, had come out cleansed. So he then threw his whole body into the mire. He emerged with his skin white and clear. He had been cured.

He set forth for home, rejoicing in his recovery. But when he reached his father's court no one recognised him. He was ragged, thin and unkempt. And his face bore little resemblance to those disfigured features of the leprous Prince Bladud who had departed some years before. How could this bedraggled herdsman be of royal blood? Bladud felt rejected and was about to leave his family for ever. But then he remembered his mother's ring. He produced it and the Queen recognised it at once. This indeed was her son! What a miracle that he had been cured.

Bladud told his story and the wondrous cure became famous. The spot where it had occurred was investigated and wells were sunk. People began to arrive from all over Britain to seek the health-giving waters. Buildings appeared and the town of Bath was born.

Whether or not these happenings really occurred, it is certainly true that the waters of Bath were sacred in Celtic times. Long before the Romans arrived in the first century AD the site that is now the city centre was a revered pagan shrine. It was here that the goddess Sulis Minerva dispensed miracle cures. After the Roman conquest this shrine was expanded into a proper town, called Aquae Sulis (the waters of Sulis). Stone baths were constructed, temples appeared and, with them, a forum, theatres and villas were built. By the 5th century AD, when the Romans departed, Bath was one of the most important towns in England.

For many centuries under the Saxons the city decayed and became deserted, but the coming of Christianity brought renewed interest in the health-giving waters that were found here. A monastery was eventually built and tradesmen moved into the settlement that grew up around its walls. The wool trade brought prosperity and the town, once more, became wealthy and famous. In AD 973 Edgar, the first King of all England, was crowned here – such was the town's importance. By the time of the Norman Conquest (1066) the King's Bath, the renovated Roman reservoir, was in constant use as a medicinal pool.

Throughout the medieval period, Bath continued to grow. Charles II came here in 1663 and this gave a further boost to the town's reputation. By the 18th century Bath was the most fashionable spa and leisure centre in the country. The present classical city was built largely under the auspices of John Wood, and the pleasure facilities were expanded for the most part by the master of ceremonies, Beau Nash.

The waters of Bath derive from the only hot springs in Britain. Half a million gallons a day issue forth at a constant temperature of 120°F. The water is said to be radioactive and is used today in the treatment of a variety of ailments, including rheumatic and orthopaedic conditions, skin disorders and stomach complaints. The curative qualities of these waters are now generally accepted and many people have benefited from bathing in or drinking them. The waters emerging from other parts of the Mendip Hills are not warm, but this does not necessarily mean that they are unable to bring health to those who take them. The same, or similar, minerals may be contained within them, and the same, or similar, qualities may be identified.

Behind St Julian's church, in the village of Wellow some 6 miles south of Bath, a trickle of clear water flows out from a deep hedgerow. This is all that now remains of the once famous St Julian's Well. At one time this was called the 'lucky well' for it brought good fortune and a long life to all those who drank its waters. Its origins probably go back to Celtic times.

The church was built in 1372 by the Hungerford family who lived at the old manor house nearby (situated where the old farm and village school now stand). However, it is thought this church stands on a site long revered as a shrine. Its dedication recalls that a Roman sacred place lies hereabouts – Julian being a Latin name – and that Wellow was probably a place of pilgrimage during the so-called Dark Ages. Traditionally, St Julian was honoured as the patron saint of fishermen.

It seems probable that this early Christian site was located at a spot already regarded as sacred by Celtic pagans. The well thus would have formed a focal point for pre-Christian worship, its health-giving properties bestowing upon its waters a special significance.

21

Today the healing waters of Wellow, it seems, continue to exert a 'pull' on travellers and curious tourists alike. And the mysterious story of the white lady may also be linked to this well's strange powers. It is said a ghost of a medieval lady, dressed all in white, is sometimes seen sitting beside St Julian's Well. Her appearance foretells a calamity about to befall the Hungerford family, the Lords of the Manor. Is she trying to drink the 'lucky' waters of the well, and failing so to do?

Then there is Doulting, a short distance from Shepton Mallet. This village is now famous for its building stone but was once the destination of pilgrims, for here were St Aldhelm's Well and St Agnes' Fountain – both of which gave out waters that could heal the sick and crippled.

Doulting stone is said to be one of the loveliest building materials in England. It is a white freestone, similar to that

*St Aldhelm's Well at Doulting in the late 18th century. (Somerset Archaeological and Natural History Society)*

found at Bath but harder and more durable. A form of oolitic limestone, it is quarried along the Mendip slopes immediately above the village, and has been used for centuries. Large parts of Shepton Mallet were built with Doulting stone, as were the great abbeys at Wells and Glastonbury.

In fact, the Doulting estate was given to the monks of Glastonbury Abbey in the 8th century by Ine, King of Wessex. Even then Doulting stone was much prized as a building material, and the monks used it when they rebuilt their monastery under St Dunstan. King Ine had a special affinity for Doulting, since it was here in AD 709 that his brother Aldhelm died.

Aldhelm was a great and holy man. As the first Bishop of Sherborne, he made frequent preaching expeditions throughout Somerset and Dorset, but it was for his knowledge, generosity and simple lifestyle that he was loved by Englishmen everywhere. He was the first English cleric to write Latin verses and he designed an organ that became the father of our present church instrument. It was during one of his expeditions, which he undertook on foot, that he fell ill. He came here to Doulting to seek the curative waters but, sadly, he was too late. He died on a simple stone slab in a little wooden chapel that stood where the church now stands.

Soon Doulting became a place of pilgrimage as people came both to honour the memory of Aldhelm and to bathe in the healing waters of the well that was situated close by the chapel where the great man had died. Henceforward the well became known as St Aldhelm's Well and monks came here to read psalms and say prayers over the hallowed site.

Even before Aldhelm's day, however, the waters had long been revered for possessing healing properties. They could cure paralysis, nervous tics, rashes and such diseases as shingles. They could even rid cattle of various animal ailments including 'quarter-ail', a form of palsy. In Celtic times a pagan temple was built hereabouts to enable those cured to thank the water gods. Later the village became a regular stopping point for cattle drovers, who brought any sick animals to the waters.

Today the double spring, which marks the site of St

*St Aldhelm's Well at Doulting today.*

Aldhelm's Well, can be found below the church, close to the back of the vicarage garden. The waters are channelled through a wall to feed the old village well. Nearby, where the village pump once stood, is another spring, once called St Agnes' Fountain. This also provided healing waters and was used during busy periods by those pilgrims unable to reach St Aldhelm's Well.

The Dissolution of the Monasteries may have led to the well and fountain being smashed up but the 'pull' of the waters continued. As recently as the 19th century people were coming to Doulting to take the cures. The headmaster of Shepton Mallet school, John Farbrother, wrote that he had heard tell 'of a late, learned divine who was in the habit of walking thither from Shepton, regularly every morning, for the purpose of bathing his eyes, and whose sight was said to have been much benefited thereby.'

The cult of water worship can be found throughout the world and in all historic periods. The ancient Egyptians and Greeks venerated water, as did the peoples of the old empires of the East – the Chinese, the Mongols and Mesopotamians. In the tribes of North America and tropical Africa there is the tradition of the water cult as there is too amongst the aboriginal peoples of the southern continents.

In Britain, also, by Celtic times, water was a well-established part of pagan philosophy. It was seen, rightly, as a life force, a giver of energy and a crucible of creation. It was considered almost as a living creature. In consequence, water took on the quality of a deity, being revered either as a god itself or as the bringer of the power of the gods. In Welsh the word 'llygad' meant both 'source of a river' and 'eye'. The sources of rivers – that is, springs and wells – were seen as the eyes of the gods. The old saying 'you must not look into running water because you look into God's eye' is probably a throw-back to those pagan times when water had an ethereal quality.

'Holy wells' and 'healing wells' became almost synonymous – for the wells that were possessed by the gods would cure the ailments of those who worshipped at the shrines. Temples were built above healing wells and those springs which had certain medicinal properties were endowed with holy powers also. From earliest times, water was linked with sacred practices and so acquired its own symbolism and ritual. It assumed miraculous qualities and could cure a variety of illnesses. Some wells were given, or possessed, specific healing powers, curing a single disease perhaps. Others were thought to cure almost anything from toothache to tumours, from dumbness to dropsy. Eye sores were the most common ailments said to be cured by holy wells, perhaps because of the link between water and the 'eyes of the gods'. But other problems also featured regularly. Infertility could be treated, as could baldness, ugliness and lameness. Various skin complaints received the water treatment, as did epilepsy, asthma, colic, piles and gout. There was, indeed, hardly an illness that did not have a cure at some well or other.

How the water from these wells and springs was taken varied. Sometimes it was drunk, sometimes it was dabbed on the skin over the afflicted parts of a person's body. At some places the pilgrims had to immerse themselves in the water, partially or totally. It was also customary for people to leave offerings – a pin, a pebble, an item of clothing or some money. These represented gifts to the gods. At some wells flowered decorations would be hung about, perhaps once a year on certain sacred days. This custom of 'dressing' a well was especially common in Derbyshire but was also found here in Somerset.

The water cult continued into the Christian era and, indeed, the early Christian missionaries often transferred the old pagan wells into places of Christian worship. Many old Celtic well chapels were turned into baptistries and the tradition of water immersion was incorporated into the Christian ritual. Some of the ancient healing wells were re-dedicated to Christian saints and those saints themselves were given the credit for the cures produced by the waters. Even the Reformation of the 16th century and Puritanism of the 17th century were unable to extinguish fully the power and pull of these ancient water sites. People continued to visit wells and springs and continued to bring gifts to the mystic powers. The 'wishing well' of today is a direct descendant of the pagan healing well. The wish may be seen as a secular prayer, the coins as a gift to the water gods.

It must be asked if these ancient beliefs are based only on superstition. Without examples of people actually being healed by wells or springs the confidence in healing waters could surely not have lasted so long. Some say that any cures that do occur after a visit to a well may be attributed to psychological factors – because the pilgrims believed they would get better, they did, as a result of the so-called 'placebo effect'. But there are numerous instances of water cures being successfully administered to animals, and in such cases psychological factors can hardly be suggested.

So what is the truth? Assuming healing waters really do heal, what are the reasons for their power? Do the waters actually contain elements which act upon a body or do they stimulate the body's own intrinsic healing abilities?

The medical profession now accepts the healing qualities of the waters of Bath. The hot springs, it is now agreed, really do ease bodily pains and help in the fight against rheumatic illness and orthopaedic ailments. How long will it be before the medical profession accepts the reality of the other healing waters of Mendip?

Spa waters, it is recognised, have therapeutic qualities that can be divided into three categories. First there are saline waters, in which magnesium sulphate and other salts help the body fight inflammations and congestive disorders, like dropsy, gout and liver complaints. Salt is also said to relieve cramp and fight gangrenous infections. Secondly, there are chalybeate waters, which are reddish in colour and contain iron. These are used in tonics and in the treatment of anaemia. Thirdly, there are sulphur waters, which are used for tackling skin complaints, rheumatism and arthritis. The waters of Bath fall into this category.

As for the other healing waters of Mendip – into which category do they fall, if any? Or are the real qualities of these particular wells and springs yet to be discovered?

# 3

# WINDS OVER WINDWHISTLE

The continuing mystery of the turbulent
skies of south Somerset

Windwhistle Hill, at the southern tip of Somerset, is a
wondrous place. It stands over 700 ft above sea level and
from its long, ridge-like summit two coastlines can be seen.
To the north, on clear days, the Bristol Channel is visible
across the Somerset Levels. To the south the English Channel
can be glimpsed over the Devon hills, down the valley of the
river Axe. This upland escarpment has a complicated
geology, being made of sandstone, limestone and greensand,
and is covered by a dense woodland of tall beech trees. In
autumn the prospect is glorious and the area is justifiably
popular with tourists. Below the hill lies Cricket St Thomas,
the famous wildlife park and leisure complex, and a little to
the north stands the old market town of Ilminster. All around
is a lovely, unspoilt countryside of wooded combes, ancient
woodlands and quiet, half-forgotten villages.

But Windwhistle has a more sinister side and holds many
strange secrets. The place is well named. The winds seem
always to be whistling about the dark treetops and the air
appears ever turbulent over the whale-backed summit. Even
on calm days the woodlands stir; even when the skies are
blanket-blue to the far horizons, clouds rumble about the
rugged ridge. Strange sights have been seen above
Windwhistle – bright lights, figures and shapes. Odd sounds
have been heard and weird sensations have numbed the
lonely traveller. What mysteries surround this place? What
mystical phenomena are to be experienced? And why?

*The tall beech trees of Windwhistle.*

The first documented evidence of strange sightings appeared in a book called *Mirabilis Annus* – the Year of Wonders – published in the late 17th century. This catalogued a number of reports that were made during the year 1662 by the people of Chard and Crewkerne, the towns situated at either end of Windwhistle Hill. What was interesting about these reports was that the sightings described were common to the whole population living in the area. Most UFO observations seem to be made by individuals or small groups of people, in which instances corroboration can be difficult. But in the cases listed by *Mirabilis Annus* the phenomena were universally seen by the people living in south Somerset.

On the 12th July in that year, towards evening, two suns appeared in the sky at the same time. Two days later, at about 10 pm, three moons appeared concurrently. Five days after that – on the 19th July – two suns were seen again. On the following day, the 20th, an even stranger sight was recorded. About an hour after sunset, above the village of Chillington which lies under the northern slopes of Windwhistle, a long blue cloud billowed up from the west. Out of the swirling vapour a figure appeared – a man with a rod in his hand. He was the size of a giant. For a while he remained motionless and silent, then he vanished. Soon after, another giant appeared, this time a man on horseback. He was wearing a flat, round bonnet and was carrying a sword in his hand. Beside him a long sheaf, shaped like a feather, was hanging from his belt. Soon he vanished, too. Then followed the most curious sight of all. An entire battle was re-enacted in the clouds. The whole sky was filled with giant, ghostly figures. Several companies of horse and foot soldiers marched towards each other. One army approached from the east, the other from the west. Then they charged. The soldiers were dressed in armour and armed with muskets, the horses were draped for battle. The sights and sounds of the fight were muffled but it was without doubt a ferocious encounter. After some while – the report was not specific about how long – all went quiet. The figures faded and the clouds dispersed. The skies became silent and clear.

The suns and moons, seen on the 12th, 14th and 19th of July, might possibly be explained away as comets or prismatic tricks of the light in the turbulent atmosphere, but how can the battle scene witnessed on the 20th be justified? One theory is that it was a kind of mirage. After the sun had set over the Blackdown Hills, so it is argued, the heat haze over the Somerset Levels cooled, causing atmospheric disturbance. In the shimmering air that resulted, a scene that was taking place elsewhere was reflected up and over the horizon. What the people of south Somerset might have seen, in fact, was a battle that was being fought somewhere far away, beyond Europe maybe. But this explanation suggests that such mirages can occur clearly over thousands of miles and can produce realistic figures. Also, history records no such battle taking place on that day, anywhere, that would have resembled the scene. Other theories, linking the phenomena to the aurora borealis (the luminous northern lights), seem equally far-fetched. So what did cause these strange sightings?

Further weird visions have been seen since the 17th

century, as we shall discover, but nothing since then has been so spectacular. Some, although spine-chilling, are almost prosaic by comparison.

During the 17th and 18th centuries the countryside around Windwhistle was a favourite spot for highwaymen. The road that ran along the ridge, now the A30, was an important coaching route from London to the West Country. Travellers heading for Exeter and beyond would journey up from Crewkerne to the summit and then turn left down the line of the old Roman road, the Foss Way. This took them via Tatworth and Axminster to the south Devon coast road, thus avoiding the steep Snowdon Hill outside Chard. Highwaymen, therefore, would hide in wait amongst the beech trees, hidden from sight, until the carriages passed by with their rich cargoes. It is said that the Windwhistle Inn – a tavern still to be found near the Windwhistle summit – was the headquarters for these highwaymen. No stranger with money, the story is told, could enter this inn and come out alive. The wells and caves that dot the Windwhistle hillside were used by the highwaymen, not only to hide their booty but also to dispose of the bodies of those they had slain. Not

*The Windwhistle Inn today.*

31

a few skeletons have been discovered in these hideouts over the years.

Many of the residents of south Somerset believe these highwaymen still haunt the lanes of Windwhistle. When the wind blows and the trees bend, and the moon disappears behind a cloud, the shouts and cries of the sad victims can still be heard. Gunshots and screams ring out in the night air. Many a motorist has heard the tap-tap-tap on his car window as a ghostly highwayman knocks with his horse-crop. A disembodied hand has been seen hovering above the roadway in a luminous haze. The story goes that a highwayman once stopped a coach by grasping the window frame with his hand. But one of the occupants, armed for such an eventuality, was holding a hatchet, and brought the blade down swiftly on the assailant's wrist. The horrified highwayman managed to escape but he left his hand behind. And still that hand remains, to freeze the blood of lonely travellers on the Windwhistle road.

But it was not just highwaymen who roamed the slopes of Windwhistle Hill. Smugglers also travelled this way. They shipped in the contraband cargo at nearby Seaton and Lyme Regis and brought it via Axminster to the secret hiding places to be found either side of the Foss Way. Under cover of

darkness they would reach the isolated villages of Chillington, Cudworth, Chaffcombe and Purtington. There they would hide their 'free trade' goods in the cellars of the cottages until it was time to transport them onwards, by cart, to the distant markets of Bath, Bristol and Salisbury. Sometimes the customs men might follow the bootleggers inland and pounce when they thought they had a good chance of overpowering their prey. Should they fail, they rarely stayed alive. Dead men tell no tales and the smugglers had, at all costs, to keep secret their hiding places.

The fights between customs men and smugglers continue to be witnessed, for the souls of such men remain restless. Many a time do those who live around Windwhistle hear the shouts of a phantom tussle, with the rumble of the booty carts and the gallop of hooves. Down in the valley at Combe the clash of swords and the repeat of gunshot is a common sound, and the cries of dying men frequently fill the night-time air.

Other strange sounds can follow the winds over Windwhistle, and other strange sights can accompany the moon. Down near Cricket Malherbie the ghost of a love-lorn boy haunts the lonely crossroads. This particular young man, from Cricket St Thomas, fell in love with a beautiful girl who lived at Cricket Court. The couple used to meet secretly at these crossroads. But the girl's two brothers found out and followed the couple one night to their roadside tryst. There they murdered their sister's suitor and buried him in the nearby ditch. But still today the crying sobs of a young man can be heard and the apparition of a sad, lonely figure can be seen.

At nearby Cudworth another ghost is sometimes heard. At the vicarage a tumbling noise can break the silence, as if a body is falling down a wooden staircase. But no staircase exists in that part of the house, not any more. The present stairs have been relocated. But it was down the original steps that someone once fell. Many years ago a man was killed by his brother, who pushed him downstairs in a fit of rage. The body still falls from time to time, as the soul of the victim continues to search for a lasting rest.

Over the years, people have believed that it is in this lonely, romantic and uncanny countryside that witches reside and that this is a place where the Devil tempts the witless traveller. But it has not always been so. Once upon a time this part of south Somerset was well-populated and busy, a positive hub of human activity. What a mysterious change has come over the landscape!

Being situated on the Foss Way and on the main route from London to the West Country (now the A30), Windwhistle Hill was for a long time the focal point for trade and travellers. By medieval times the villages which had sprung up on either side were all thriving and an annual fair had been set up at White Down, at the western end. Each community boasted its own church and manor house, and the fair attracted dealers from as far afield as Cornwall, South Wales and Hampshire. By the 16th century the area had become very wealthy indeed, the villages being occupied in butter and cheese making, milling, weaving and glove manufacture. The fair was by then a four-day event held each Whitsuntide. But today all this activity seems to have disappeared. The villages are little more than hamlets, and the site of the White Down Fair is now occupied by a golf course. So what happened?

The enclosure movement, when the commons were hedged for sheep grazing and the peasants were removed from their rural hovels, put paid to many of the settlements. The occasional plague, endemic for a long time after the Black Death of the 14th century, also decimated their populations. At Cricket St Thomas the extension of the parkland, once owned by the Hood family, led to many of the cottages being demolished, to make way for more expansive garden designs during the 18th century. At Cudworth a large number of the old businesses closed as the nearby towns of Chard and Crewkerne grew. By the 19th century the area had become as deserted as it is today.

But could there have been another reason for the depopulation of the Windwhistle district? Could it have been that so many strange happenings occurred that people became scared and left the area? The lights and shapes in the skies, the evil activities of smugglers and highwaymen and, since those days, the odd ghostly sightings – could it be that these have led to the landscape becoming empty?

As for the strange lights in the sky, were they UFOs or can science provide an explanation? Could they, perhaps, be attributed to comets and meteorites?

Comets can be described as light balls in the solar system which are created by particles enveloped by layers of tenuous gas. Some of these balls, the largest, have 'tails' and can be very bright indeed, seen easily by the naked eye. Others are small and appear merely as bright spots in the night sky. Meteors are particles, like dust or sand, which move around space at random; meteorites are particles which come from space to earth, some of these crashing onto the earth's surface as rocks. Meteors and meteorites frequently occur in groups, creating 'storms'.

Comets travel periodically, at set time sequences. The most famous, Halley's Comet, passes across the earth's field of vision every 76 years, but larger ones can travel in more infrequent timescales – perhaps thousands or even millions of years separating their appearance. These larger comets, of course, cannot be predicted by scientists. If the suns and moons seen over Windwhistle in 1662 had been a comet, or comets, then it may be the first and last time such sightings could be possible during man's existence on earth.

The size and scale of comets can be hard to assess, but it is thought that the largest in the universe could be 50 kilometres in diameter. At any one time comets of this size can enter the solar system and be destroyed by the heat of the sun. When they split up they may cause meteor storms, creating strange patterns of light in the night skies. When a meteor comes to earth, as a meteorite, the devastation can be enormous. In June 1908 one large meteorite crashed into remote Siberia, in an area of tundra, covered by swamps, pine forests and peat bogs, and roamed by nomadic herdsmen. Accordingly, not much was known about the actual destruction caused locally. But its effects were certainly seen over a wider area. So big was the fireball, it was spotted from a distance of 1,000 miles. The night skies over the whole of

Europe were lit up. In England, 3,000 miles away, it was possible to play cricket at night-time. It is thought that it was a similar disaster, but on a larger scale, that destroyed the dinosaurs about 65 million years ago. At that time, a meteorite, thought to have been 12 miles wide, crashed into an area now occupied by the Yucatan peninsula in Mexico. The resulting fall-out, a sulphur cloud blacking out the sun for up to 30 years, led to a mini Ice Age. In such cold conditions the dinosaurs could not survive.

So comets, meteors and meteorites could be responsible for a number of the lights in our skies – and, indeed, for some of the other weird phenomena experienced over Windwhistle. But what of the air-bound battles, the ghostly figures, the wind-blown phantoms?

Michael Persinger, an American professor of psychology and neuroscience, has devised a theory that might explain many paranormal experiences. Essentially, this theory links geological instability with unusual brain activity. Earthquakes, says Persinger, can create powerful electromagnetic fields in the atmosphere. Not only do these cause luminous apparitions in the swirling air currents, but also they can cause interruptions in the brain's normal process. 'Temporal lobe stimulation', as this phenomenon is called, can give people an unreal feeling, with disorientated perceptions. Bright lights and shapes may be seen, and any number of apparent movements in a night sky.

So, could the complicated geology underneath Windwhistle be causing a swirl of magnetic, seismic forces? And, if so, could these give rise to those mysterious visions in the air? Or is there another, less scientific, explanation?

# 4

# THE REAL DOONES OF EXMOOR

The mystery of 17th-century
Badgworthy – fact or legend?

The gang forced its way into a lonely farmhouse near Martinhoe, in the wilds of Exmoor. Christopher Babcock's young wife was there with their infant son, and their maid was in the kitchen. The villains snatched the babe from its mother's arms and threw it down onto the lime-ash floor. Then some of their number carried off the poor woman, crying and shrieking, whilst the others ransacked the house. But when they found neither food nor valuables they grew angry and violent. They picked up the baby and tossed it to one another, shouting and laughing as they did so. They chanted nursery rhymes – 'Ride a cock horse to Banbury Cross' and 'Bye-bye baby bunting'. But it was no game they were playing. The child was dashed against the cold, hard floor. The maid, who had hidden herself in the oven in fear for her life, heard the callous voices ring out:

> 'If any man asketh who killed thee
> Say 'twas the Doones of Bagworthy.'

This story is told by R.D. Blackmore in his novel *Lorna Doone*, which was published in 1869. The book was set in 17th-century Exmoor and told of the love of John Ridd for the young Lorna Doone, adopted daughter of the wicked Doone family which lived at Bagworthy. It was an exciting and romantic tale set against the wild and beautiful landscape of Somerset's western borders.

Today *Lorna Doone* is considered one of the classics of English literature and many tourists come to Exmoor because of the book's links with this part of the West Country. The village of Malmsmead is a popular spot for visitors, for it stands at the end of the valley drained by Badgworthy Water, an area named even on Ordnance Survey maps as 'Doone Country'. Oare church, a few miles east of Malmsmead, is another favourite tourist destination, being the place where a famous incident occurred in the book – the shooting by Carver Doone of Lorna as she was about to marry John Ridd. Close by is Robber's Bridge, another place connected with the Doones and popular with visitors. In fact, all over Exmoor there are places associated with the story of Lorna Doone and her wicked family.

But did the Doones really exist? Did R.D. Blackmore base his novel on certain factual stories or was the whole tale completely made up? In the book Blackmore gives a concise history of the Doone family, explaining how it had originated in Scotland and why it had settled in this inhospitable corner of Somerset. How true is that history? Blackmore adds certain footnotes under particular descriptions of Doone infamy, saying 'This story is strictly true' and 'This vile deed was done, beyond all doubt'. But were these footnotes themselves ingredient parts of the novel, added by the author to give authenticity to his saga? Or were they honest attempts by Blackmore to show that the story was indeed based on fact?

Perhaps we should start our investigation by giving the first word to Blackmore himself. At the front of his novel he wrote a preface, and this should be read with care. It could give us our first clue. The important section of this preface runs as follows:

'This work is called a "romance", because the incidents, characters, time and scenery, are alike romantic. And in shaping this old tale, the Writer neither dares, nor desires, to claim for it the dignity or cumber it with the difficulty of an historic novel.

And yet he thinks that the outlines are filled in more carefully, and the situations (however simple) more warmly coloured and quickened, than a reader would expect to find

*Doone Country – and a memorial stone erected to commemorate the centenary of the publication of* Lorna Doone *in 1869.*

in what is called a "legend".

And he knows that any son of Exmoor, chancing on this volume, cannot fail to bring to mind the nurse-tales of his childhood – the savage deeds of the outlaw Doones in the depth of Bagworthy Forest . . .'

In the novel there is a brief description of the history of the Doone family and its flight from Scotland. According to this, the tale runs as follows.

In about the year 1640, when England's troubles were swelling to an outburst, great estates in the north country were being confiscated either through family feuds or through undue influence from Court. These estates were often held in co-heirship, or joint tenancy, whereby the land would pass wholly to one owner should the other owner die. Now it happened that one particular property was owned jointly by Sir Ensor Doone and his cousin, the Earl of Lorne and Dykemont. 'By wiles and woman's meddling', however, this holding was confiscated from them both, each man being expelled from the land that was rightfully his. Yet, whereas the Earl of Lorne merely had his wealth reduced, Sir Ensor Doone was totally impoverished and was left a beggar. He blamed his kinsman who, he thought, had wronged him. A fierce argument ensued. At last, being hot-headed and impetuous, Sir Ensor rode away from the district and took with him his wife and sons.

Some said Sir Ensor subsequently took his grievances to the King but did not get a fair hearing. Some said otherwise, that he killed a man at Court whom he suspected of being involved in the plunder of his fortune. Others said he insulted Charles I in a manner beyond forgiveness. But whatever the exact reason, wrote Blackmore, Sir Ensor became a felon and an outlaw. In despair he resolved to settle in some outlandish part of the country where no one would know him. In this way he came to Somerset and discovered a place withdrawn and self-defended, uneasy of access and hidden from sight. He made this his home and so Bagworthy village grew up.

At first the Doones were honest and the local countryfolk tolerated them. But, as time went by and they had more mouths to feed, they took to diverse illegal ways. They plundered and killed, they stole and kidnapped. They fell foul of their Exmoor neighbours and lived as best they could, outside the law. At first there were about a dozen of them, the Doones and their retainers. But this number grew. As Blackmore wrote, 'the Doones increased much faster than their honesty.' They carried off local women – farmers' wives and daughters – who protested at first but grew more disposed in time to their new lives: 'women like strong men more than weak ones, feeling that they need some staunchness, something to hold fast by.'

At first, the locals did nothing more than grumble, perhaps because they respected the Doones' noble birth and felt pity for the injustice they had suffered. But, after a while, matters became worse and it was too late for them to be driven from the district.

The sons of Ensor grew up haughty and full of hatred. One night they raided a house near Minehead and one of their number was killed. In revenge they murdered everybody in the building and burned it to the ground, leaving only a child with its reason gone. But this heinous crime became only the first of many as the Doones began to terrorise the neighbourhood.

Blackmore's story then continues by tracing the events surrounding Lorna Doone and her relationship with a local yeoman farmer named John Ridd. In 1673 the Doones kidnapped young Lorna, who was the daughter of their sworn enemy, the Scottish Lord Dugal, and took her back to their home at Bagworthy. She was little more than a child. The Doones gave her their surname and she grew up believing that she was, by blood, one of them. The plan was to wait until Lorna came of age. When that date arrived she would be married to Ensor's son and heir, Carver Doone, so that, in due course, the Doones would gain the Dugal inheritance.

But before Lorna became 21 she met and fell in love with John Ridd. He rescued her from the Doone Valley and carried her off to safety. The Doones went in pursuit, but soon Lorna's real identity was discovered and the Court summoned her to London. There she took her rightful position as Lady Dugal. Later on, Lorna returned to Exmoor in order to marry her sweetheart, John Ridd. The wedding took place at Oare church but during the service a shot rang out. From outside the church the wicked Carver had fired at the bride, aiming his pistol through the side window. Lorna fell to the ground injured, but she survived and with her husband John was able to live happily ever after.

Readers of *Lorna Doone* should not, of course, expect the landscapes described in the book to resemble exactly the real scenery of Exmoor. Blackmore himself admitted that the countryside of west Somerset merely inspired his writing. He exaggerated the natural features, he romanticised about the solitude, and he used poetic licence to enhance his literary descriptions.

That being said, the similarities between the Doone country of the book and the 'Doone Country' of modern maps are undeniable. This is especially true of the place that the Doones called home – Bagworthy. For this really did exist.

*Hoccombe Combe and the site of medieval Badgworthy village.*

The village was, and is, pronounced 'Badgery'. In Blackmore's novel it was spelt Bagworthy, whilst on maps the form is Badgworthy. Place-name spellings frequently differ like this. It is known that Blackmore visited the area in 1840, long before he wrote his book, and it is said he marvelled at the ruins of the tiny village here, for by then the settlement had already disappeared. On today's maps the spot is marked by the words 'Medieval Village (site of)' and will be found towards the upper reaches of Badgworthy Water, close to where the tributary stream runs down from Hoccombe Combe. By Blackmore's day probably only the foundations were visible. In the book, which after all is set two centuries earlier, the village was described as a settlement of 14 cottages, stone built, either side of the stream. All the cottages, save one, were single-storeyed.

Documentary evidence suggests that Badgworthy village had Saxon origins, its name deriving from Baga's worth meaning 'Baga's clearing'. Baga was possible the name of a local tribal leader. After the Norman Conquest the whole estate here, including nearby Brendon, was given by William I to Henry Pomerois or Pomeroy. He, in his turn, granted the land to the 'Brethren of the Hospital of St John of Jerusalem'. At that time, it seems the area now called 'Doone Country' was known as the 'land of the hermits', since it was inhabited by a small group of monks or friars. During the 14th century the Prior of the Hospital of Jerusalem gave the estate to a man called Walter, who took the surname Badgworthy. His son John passed the land on to Robert, Lord Harrington, who was Lord of the Manor at Brendon.

By 1430 the Badgworthy estate, still owned by Brendon manor, was beginning to decline. Bailiff records note that there were difficulties in letting the farms in that valley, and the moor was starting to make incursions into the once-cultivated fields. What happened thereafter is something of a mystery, since no documents survive. But we can hazard a guess. The enclosure movement, which began in Tudor times, led to the loss of many Exmoor commons where the rural poor had grazing rights. Sheep were moved into the area by the great landowners, and the scattered populations moved out. Many villages declined, Badgworthy probably being one of them.

Medieval Badgworthy was made up of cottages built in the traditional two-roomed, 'long-house' style. Each building was split crossways. One end would have been where the family lived, the other end where the animals were kept. In the 1930s Alfred Vowles, an antiquarian, counted the foundations of 14 cottages here – interestingly the same number that Blackmore mentions in *Lorna Doone*. Thus we can safely assume that Badgworthy in the Middle Ages was probably a mean hamlet with some 50 to 100 inhabitants, bearing in mind the average size of families in those days.

And who lived at Badgworthy? A few hard-pressed farmers, no doubt, with their impoverished dependants. There is a story that the very last inhabitant was a man called Tucker, who lived there at the beginning of the 19th century. But he died one night with his little granddaughter, when a blizzard cut them off as they walked home from Simonsbath. Some years after that supposed incident, a shepherd's cottage was built further up the valley, the stones for this being taken from the Badgworthy ruins. That cottage is now called 'Lorna's Cot' but it has nothing to do with the story of Lorna Doone.

Badgworthy, therefore, was once a small, isolated village which gave shelter to a few hardy souls. Could it have been the home, in the 17th century, of a family called Doone?

Interestingly, the tradition that a gang of villains once lived there goes back to a time before Blackmore wrote his novel. *Lorna Doone* was published in 1869, but certain other writings pre-date that book and these also mention the Doones. The Vicar of Lynton in the 1840s, the Reverend Matthew Mundy, collected many of the Doone stories and had them written out by the girls of Lynton National School. The essays were published in 1853. In the same year the *Guide to Lynton* appeared, written by T.H. Cooper. This contained a whole section on the 'Doones of Badgworthy', chronicling the evil doings of this most notorious of families. Four years later, in 1857, there appeared another literary effort – an article in *Fraser's Magazine* written by the Reverend George Tugwell and entitled 'Wanderings on Exmoor'. This was especially interesting, since it retold in detail many of the legends of Exmoor. Amongst these were some references to the Doones. At one point Tugwell describes a night he spent around a cottage peat-fire, smoking a pipe with a man who had been born and bred on the moor. They sat together on the oaken settle and the cottager told his story. The article included the following extract:

'We do not forget with what seriousness he told us of that fierce gang of marauders infamous in moorland story, the Doones of Badgworthy, at whose name Exmoor children quake, and repent them full sore of all their evil deeds. How these ancient freebooters (whose stronghold is pointed out to the passenger in a wild part of the moor, on the boundary line of Devon and Somerset), one dark night suddenly appeared before a lone barton, or homestead, in an unfrequented beat of their country, and burst through the frail protections of bolt and door – being aware, like brave men as they were, that the farmer and his servants were at work in their distant fields. But there was a little child and a servant girl remaining, whose fate was quickly determined.'

This article went on to describe much the same story that Blackmore told in *Lorna Doone*, retold at the beginning of this chapter. The question then arises, did Blackmore write of a well-known incident or did he take his story from Tugwell's article?

It certainly appears from the above-mentioned writings, which were published before *Lorna Doone*, that numerous tales were circulating in the 19th century about a gang of villains called Doone living in the 17th century. These tales had the common elements of robbery, kidnapping and murder. In one account the Doones killed a baby whilst singing an evil-worded couplet. In another, they broke into a farmhouse and murdered all the inhabitants, children and mother included. One version of this latter story has the Doones accompanied by an old hag. When they burst into the farmhouse they found the child in its cot and the mother in hiding. 'Kill the calf and the cow will howlee', cried the hag. So the Doones put a sword to the baby, forcing the mother out from her hiding place. Seeing her baby killed, the poor woman broke down and told the Doones where the valuables were kept. They gathered these items up and then murdered the mother as well. On the following day, it was said, a great dog appeared and lapped up the blood that still lay about the cottage. It was a dog belonging to the Doones.

However, whilst the various tales of their crimes had much in common there seemed to be little agreement in these legends about the Doone family origins. Some said they were dispossessed cavaliers who had been forced into crime after the Civil War. Others said they were refugees from the Duke of Monmouth's forces, which had been heavily defeated at the battle of Sedgemoor. But in both these cases the dates seem not to tally. The Civil War took place between 1642 and 1649 and the battle of Sedgemoor was fought in 1685. The Doones, however, appear to have settled in Exmoor before 1640.

Another theory about the Doone background was proposed by Dr Francis C. Eeles towards the end of the

19th century. He said that the graveyard behind St Dubricius' church, Porlock, contained the tomb of Adam Bellenden and that this was the clue. Bellenden had been Bishop of Aberdeen and Chancellor of Aberdeen University. He was given the living of Porlock by Charles I and died there in 1647. He had come originally from Dunblane in Scotland, a place which was close to another village called Doune. Bellenden, suggested Eeles, brought with him to Somerset a servant who was from that village of Doune and who had taken on that name as his own. When Bellenden died, this servant, left friendless and poor, turned to crime, moving into the depths of Exmoor to continue his newly-acquired occupation.

This may be a fanciful theory, but it is interesting in one respect. It links the Doone family with Scotland.

On the 12th October 1901 an interesting, if rather curious, article appeared in the *West Somerset Free Press*, entitled 'A Short History of the Original Doones of Exmoor. Their Descent and Reason for their Exile'. The piece was written by a certain Ida Marie Browne, who signed herself 'Audrie Doon'. She claimed that she was the great-great-great-granddaughter of Charles Doone, eldest son of Ensor and thus the original Carver Doone.

In the article Ida Browne claimed to be descended through her mother's line, her mother's maiden name being Doon. The terminal 'e' in the name, she asserted, was added in earlier times but the original spelling had been Doune. It was her ancestors the Dounes who had been exiled from Scotland in 1620, had settled in the Oare valley, where they became 'more or less hated and feared by the countryside', and had returned to their native Perthshire in 1699. The full details about Sir Ensor's departure from Scotland were given.

In 1618, wrote Ida Browne, Sir Ensor James Doune was imprisoned by his kinsman the Earl of Moray, on whose estates he laid claim. Sir Ensor and the Earl (Sir James Stuart and nicknamed the 'Bonny Earl of Moray') were twins and held joint ownership of Doune Castle and its estates, situated near Stirling in Perthshire. But the two had fallen out. The Earl claimed sole ownership and Ensor was given a choice.

Either he could remain in prison or else he could leave Scotland for ever. He chose the latter course. Accordingly, he came to England, accompanied by his wife and a servant, a man called Beeton. At the Court of King James I, however, Sir Ensor failed to find any sympathy for his grievances. He was a proud, vindictive and quarrelsome man and took this rebuff to heart. He thus determined to take revenge upon the world that had so wronged him.

He and his family travelled west from London and eventually came upon Exmoor, where the landscape reminded him of his native Scotland. By the East Lyn valley he took possession of a half-ruined farmhouse. As time went by sons were born to the outlawed knight. These sons inherited their father's stern, unbending nature and his violent temper. They grew up to see all other men as enemies.

For the rest of the century the Doone family terrorised their Exmoor neighbourhood. They raided farms, robbed travellers, stole animals and murdered all those who stood in their way. Eventually, however, in 1699, their sordid way of life came to an abrupt end. The new Earl of Moray repented the wrongs committed by his grandfather. He asked the Doones back to Scotland and offered reparation. The family accepted this olive branch and so left Exmoor for ever. In conclusion, Ida Browne surmised that Blackmore must have heard the Doone story from some Scottish friends and transferred its essential elements to his novel. He merely changed some of the names.

Many people were sceptical of Ida Browne's article, and asserted that she had invented the whole thing. Neither the *Peerage of Scotland* nor *Burke's Peerage*, they said, made any mention that the Bonny Earl of Moray had a twin brother. They also said that no documents anywhere mentioned the name 'Sir Ensor Doune', and no records existed about any land quarrels involving the Earls of Moray. The sceptics were equally dismissive about other so-called 'evidence'. An old journal still existed, written by a certain Rupert Doone in the 1740s, that seemed to suggest that the author's forebears had been Exmoor villains. But this could have been faked. Also, a certain John William Beeton of Hunstanton in Norfolk claimed to be a descendant of the Dounes' servant, and said that he had owned some Doone 'relics', including a large oil painting of Sir Ensor Doone dated 1679, and a flintlock pistol engraved 'C. Doone 1681' on one side of the butt and 'Porlock C.D.' on the other. But many of these relics were later accidentally destroyed by fire – conveniently so, according to the doubters.

One of the principal sceptics, who saw the Doone legend merely as a fictional account developed by Blackmore and based on the slenderest of rumours, was Edwin John Rawle. He was a native of Exmoor and, indeed, his family had lived on the Somerset-Devon borders since pre-Reformation times. His grandfather had been born at Oareford in 1768, and his father in 1805. If anyone should have heard about the Doones it would have been the Rawles. Yet they had not come across stories of them until after *Lorna Doone* was published.

E.J. Rawle spent his childhood fishing the Badgworthy and Oare Waters and never once, said he, did any mention of the Doones reach his ears. In about 1880 he met an old inhabitant, one William Lock, who was then about 90 years old. The old man told Rawle that he had 'never heard tell of any robbers or Doones about Oare till few years back'. This led Rawle to search further into the Doone story. Accordingly, he studied all the county archives and every parish record. No mention did he find anywhere of the Doones. He published his findings in 1893 (*The Annals of Exmoor Forest*) and concluded that the Doones were totally fictional. Blackmore at that time was still alive – he died in 1900 – but never did he contact Rawle to contradict his conclusion.

In 1903 Rawle published a further work about his research into the Doones – a book entitled *The Doones of Exmoor*. In this he put forward his own theory about the origin of the Doone legend. Exmoor, he wrote, was a wild, remote landscape where 'bogey' tales easily became exaggerated. Parents would make their children behave with stories about vicious gangs roaming the moors, and landowners would scare their tenants with threats of mysterious reprisals if they

*Badgworthy Water near Oare Common.*

did not pay their rents. During the 17th and 18th centuries Exmoor was also an area where smugglers plied their illegal trade. Contraband would be carried by packhorse from the secret caves and inlets along the coast to lonely farms and cottages inland where it could be stored, safely away from prying eyes. Rawle surmised that it was probably the smugglers themselves who deliberately circulated the story of the Doones, expanding on an existing oral tradition. How better to keep people indoors at night, when they were moving their booty, than to spread tales about villains on the loose?

The legends which the smugglers elaborated, continued Rawle, were probably ancient indeed. During the so-called Dark Ages the Vikings made several raids in the West Country, and the defending Saxons had but limited success in containing their advance. The Vikings burned down many a port, including Watchet and Porlock, and set up many a settlement along the coastlands. Here and there place-names still remind us of those days – Danes Fields, Danes Cross, Danes Lane and so on. According to Rawle, it is probable that the Saxon descendants of Exmoor remembered the ruthless slaughter done by the Danes and retold the tales of savagery down through the ages. And, as is usual with oral tradition, deeds became exaggerated and names changed. Eventually the 'Danes' of the old stories became the 'Doones' of legend, and so the embryo of Blackmore's tale was formed.

This theory may seem convincing. It fits the few known facts – the existence of illegal groups in 17th-century Exmoor and the supposed local name of 'Doone' – and also accounts for the absence of any real evidence that a particular family of villains ever lived on the Somerset borders. Yet some historical facts remain outstanding. Badgworthy, or Bagworthy, really did exist as a village and probably was inhabited by a group of vagrants during the 17th century. R.D. Blackmore, himself the son of a onetime rector of Oare and Combe Martin and therefore a man who had grown up with Exmoor tales, assured his readers that his account of the Doones was based on true happenings. There was little reason for him to lie. Then we have some old writings, that pre-date the publication of *Lorna Doone*, which refer specifically to the Doone legends, together with the testimony of some Doone family descendants. How can all these pieces of evidence be fitted into the Rawle theory?

Barry Gardner published a little volume in 1989 called *Who was Lorna Doone?* This was written for the Anglo-American Lorna Doone Society, a privately funded research organisation founded in New Hampshire during the 1920s. In this booklet Gardner discusses at length the story behind the novel, the upbringing of R.D. Blackmore himself, the family connections of the character Lorna Doone, and the origins of the Doone family legend. It all makes fascinating reading. Contained in this volume is a theory that might be considered the final solution.

It seems, according to Gardner, that Blackmore drew inspiration for his novel from two sources – his own memories of the Exmoor legends and the stories told to him when young by his aunt and uncle, Mary and Richard Gordon. Richard Doddridge Blackmore was born in 1825 in Berkshire but spent much of his boyhood in west Somerset, where his father was a rector. In fact, the Blackmores had lived in Exmoor since the 17th century, owning estates there. So young Richard grew up surrounded by the legends of the Doones, which he evidently found enthralling. When he was older, however, he moved to Oxfordshire to live with his aunt Mary and her husband, the Reverend Richard Gordon, as his widowed father had remarried. The Gordons were a long established Scottish family and Uncle Richard would often tell his young nephew Richard stories about his ancestors. The Gordons were connected to the clan Dugal, which had once ruled that part of Argyllshire known as Lorne.

So, it seems, in later years when Blackmore wrote his famous novel he combined the Gordon chronicles with traditional Exmoor legends. He gave his heroine the name 'Lorna' and based her background on the Gordon-Dugal line. For the exploits of the Doones he moved the timescale forward to the 1640s onwards. This allowed him, for good literary reasons, to set his novel against the background of the English Civil War and the battle of Sedgemoor. The real Doones, wrote Gardner, actually arrived in Exmoor in the early 1620s.

Gardner went on to write that the history of the Doones as told by Ida Browne, in her article for the *West Somerset Free Press*, was not so very far from the truth. The trouble was that she had made a few fundamental errors, and these had caused sceptical readers to disbelieve the whole story. Sir Ensor Doune, or Doone, was not the twin brother of the Bonny Earl of Moray, but he was a wronged Scottish nobleman. His real name was Sir James Stewart, or Stuart, the 7th Lord of Innermeath.

The confusion arose because Sir James Stewart was a cousin, and not the brother, of Sir James Stuart, Earl of Moray. But the two men did not only share the same name, they shared the same looks. They were 'twins' in the old sense – they were a duplicate of each other. The story runs that Sir James of Innermeath had been left his estates to hold jointly with four female cousins. But those cousins treated him ill and did him out of his inheritance. The case went before the Crown but the King found in the women's favour.

Sir James was stripped of his titles and imprisoned in Edinburgh Castle. No wonder Blackmore wrote in *Lorna Doone* about the 'wiles and woman's meddling'!

At a later date Sir James was released. Bitter and resentful, he came to England and, in due course, found himself in Exmoor. There he set himself up as the head of a family gang that proceeded to behave in a manner of which legends are made. There are no documents that mention 'Sir Ensor Doone' because that was not his real name. But there is ample evidence to prove the existence and background of Sir James Stewart, Lord Innermeath. So how did the name 'Sir Ensor Doone' arise?

Barry Gardner offers an answer to this question too. It seems that when Sir James Stewart was released from prison he found himself alone. His wife had left him and his family had disowned him. He was an outcast. Shortly afterwards he took up with a woman called Margaret MacGregor. At that time the MacGregors themselves were little more than outlaws. Their lands had been seized by the Grants and the Campbells and their clan chiefs had taken to the Scottish hills to live as best they could from the barren landscape.

Mary MacGregor introduced Sir James to these chieftains and they taught him the ways of their existence. He joined their number. Each chieftain was known by a gaelic nickname – one, for example, was called Ruadh ('the red'), another was called Aluin ('the handsome'). Soon Sir James was given his own gaelic handle – Iain Ciar Duine (James 'the dusky one') – and by this did he become known.

In 1613 the MacGregors were finally defeated by their foes and the clan disbanded. Sir James and Margaret MacGregor came to England and, after failing to have their grievances aired in London, moved on to Exmoor. It seems they arrived in about the year 1623. They settled in a lonely valley near the Somerset border and lived as man and wife. Four sons were later born and Sir James found himself at the head of a family of rogues. And their name? Wishing to start life anew, Sir James called himself by his gaelic name – Sir Iain Ciar Duine. But this the locals could not pronounce properly. They called him 'Sir Ensor Doone'.

# 5

# THE WITCHES OF WINCANTON

The mystery of the pagan
heritage of witchcraft

The south-east corner of Somerset, where the hills between
Yeovil and Wincanton sweep into Dorset, is an area set apart
from the rest of the county. Both historically and culturally
it is part of Hardy's Wessex. The uplands are windswept and
treeless, the valleys are broad and empty. The few villages
that there are, like Marston Magna, Compton Pauncefoot and
Abbas Combe, nestle in a landscape that echoes to the singing
of skylarks. The marshlands of Blackmore Vale, and the wild
heaths of Bovington, are not far away.

Yet there is an undercurrent in this fair countryside – a
hidden world of superstition. Ancient customs live on and
many of the old beliefs continue to be held. Nature is still
venerated here. Witchcraft, it is said, remains a force – its
history is long and its power ever-present. Stories are told of
wizardry, and strange happenings stir the air. Wincanton was
once the traditional centre for the Somerset witches and
Yeovil was the ancient focal point for pagan festivals.
Between these two towns stood the hillfort of Cadbury
Castle, legendary site of Arthur's Camelot but in reality the
onetime capital of an Iron Age civilisation. Here, we are told,
lived the Celtic holy men – the spiritual leaders revered for
their wisdom and learning. These men were the Druids.

But what is the origin of witchcraft and who were the
witches who lived in the Wincanton area? What were the
links between their wizardry and those ancient pagan beliefs
that held Celtic tribes in thrall? And why is this corner of

Somerset, this part of Wessex, so full of the powers of nature's gods?

Witches and sorcerers, fortune-tellers and herbalists, soothsayers and oracles, such people have been recognised since the earliest times. The Ancient Egyptians and Greeks knew them, the Romans sought their services, and the Celts raised them to holy status.

The word 'witch' derives from the Anglo-Saxon word 'wicce' or 'wicche'. This referred to a person, male or female, who possessed powers of enchantment. Such people in Saxon England were neither good nor bad necessarily. Their charms or spells, such as they were, could be cast for various reasons – to secure a good harvest, for example, or bring rain to a drought or give victory in battle. Sometimes potions were prepared, or 'evil spirits' were cast out, to help the afflicted recover from illness. Such 'witches', in other words, would have been the early equivalents of those later individuals variously called 'high priests', 'medicine-men', or 'shamans'. The evil connotation of the word 'witch' was to come later.

The persecution of witches and the denunciation of witchcraft developed when Christianity became more widespread during the Middle Ages. As the churches grew in power, so those people dealing in the mysterious arts of necromancy were pushed to the sidelines of society. In 1484 Pope Innocent VIII denounced witchcraft as heretical and Roman Catholics all over Europe began to seek out and destroy all those who did not subscribe to the 'true faith'. In England the persecution of witches reached its peak in the 17th century. Henry VIII, in 1541, had made witchcraft a felony but it was not until James I came to the throne in 1603 that violent punishments were introduced.

James Stuart was obsessively against witchcraft, fervently believing witches to be creatures who had made a pact with the Devil. In 1594, when still James VI of Scotland, he had written *Daemonologie*, in which he described in detail the practices of witchcraft and the methods whereby witches could be identified. Now, as James I of England, he set forth to clear the whole country of sorcery. By Statute all persons

54

working with 'evil spirits' or indulging in witchcraft, charm or enchantment were liable to be tried. Upon conviction, they could be sentenced to death, either by hanging or else by flame, being burnt at the stake.

With a monarch so obsessed, the green light was given for all those in authority to seek out and destroy anyone suspected of witchcraft. Over-zealous magistrates everywhere tried to make a name for themselves, or to curry favour with the King, by investigating tales of sorcery and sentencing harshly all those found guilty. In 1612, for example, Roger Nowell uncovered the famous witches of Pendle in Lancashire and dealt with them accordingly. But this rampant search for sorcerers – this literal witch-hunt – did not end with James I's death. Under Charles I it continued and under Cromwell's Puritans it became even more vehement. In the 1640s the notorious Witchfinder General, Matthew Hopkins, scoured East Anglia for any signs of evil doing. His harsh treatment of the accused became legendary and sent shivers of fear around England.

Somerset had its own witch persecutor – Robert Hunt of Compton Pauncefoot, the local magistrate. During the 1660s he held a number of investigations and trials which, together, uncovered much of the hidden world of the Wincanton area. Sir Walter Scott later described Hunt as the 'Somersetshire Satan', such was his reputation. Many a poor soul went to the gallows unnecessarily because of him.

Amongst the women that Robert Hunt tried were Elizabeth Style and Alice Duke, who belonged to an alleged group of witches called Style's Knot. This coven was centred on Wincanton. Style herself lived at Stoke Trister, near Bayford on the eastern outskirts of Wincanton. The regular meetings, called 'esbats' or 'estbats', were said to have been held at nearby Leigh Common.

According to evidence given at the trial, Style's Knot had terrorised the neighbourhood for more than ten years. Thomas Garret's cows were cursed, Edith Watts was given the pox, Richard Hill's daughter was accursed with fits, Dorothy Vining was bewitched. Stories were told of weird ceremonies, of strange apparitions, of mysterious happenings.

*Stoke Trister churchyard – meeting place for the Wincanton witches.*

Thomas Conway described how Alice Duke had given him a pewter dish containing a strange oil. This, she told him, would be beneficial to his daughter. But when the liquid was anointed on his daughter's forehead, the little girl cried in pain. Suspecting a curse Mary Conway, the child's mother, threw the dish on the fire. But when it reached the flames the dish disappeared.

With such evidence, given on oath, and with Hunt's vicious cross-questioning, the accused women had little choice but to confess. Elizabeth Style herself gave a long description of how she first became a witch. Ten years before, she said, the Devil had appeared to her in the shape of a handsome man. He promised money and the pleasures of the world in return for her blood, her soul and her total obedience to his laws. She agreed and signed an agreement to that effect, writing her name on a document with the blood from the fourth finger of her right hand. The Devil then gave her sixpence and vanished. From that day on he came to her whenever she needed him. At the request of 'O Satan, give me my purpose', he would appear either as a man, a dog or a cat. When he appeared as a fly it was to suck her blood. On one particular occasion the coven met at Leigh Common to set a curse upon Elizabeth Hall. A waxen effigy was produced and the Devil appeared in the guise of a man dressed in black. He 'baptised' the effigy with oil and gave it back to the witches who then pierced it with thorns. At the close of the ceremony they all feasted on wine, cakes and roast meat which had been provided by their satanic host.

A similar description of an estbat ritual was given by Alice Duke in her testimony. She lived in Wincanton with Anne Bishop, another witch. At Marnhull, across the Dorset border, the coven met to swear allegiance to their Master. As usual he appeared as a man all dressed in black. Each witch was anointed with a greenish oil and chanted the words 'Thout tout a-tout, tout throughout and about' together with 'Rentum Tormentum'. Then music was played and they danced around. They feasted on wine, beer, meats and cakes and departed to the words 'Merry meet, merry part'.

It was a well-known belief in Somerset, during the Middle Ages, that a witch could summon the Devil by walking around a churchyard three times at midnight saying the Lord's Prayer backwards. Alice Duke, it was claimed at her trial, frequently did just that. Sometimes she was accompanied by a large black toad, sometimes by a black rat. She was also seen from time to time sitting in a trance with her black cat suckling at her breast.

Other women were also brought before Robert Hunt, accused of practising witchcraft. Margaret Agar, for example, was described as a 'rampant hag'. She lived at Brewham, east of Bruton. At her trial she told how she went about casting a spell, using a picture or effigy of her adversary and piercing its heart with a thorn. Another poor woman, Catherine Green, was accused of possessing witch items and books on enchantment. She too confessed.

Many of these witches were sent to the gallows, although Elizabeth Style herself died a natural death before she could meet the hangman. Robert Hunt's excessive treatment of witches was eventually restrained by higher authority, so the subsequent years saw a reduction in the amount of prejudice shown against the witches in the Wincanton area. But witchcraft and wizardry continued to be outlawed in other parts of England. The last execution of a witch came in 1716, at Huntingdon. It was not until 1736, in the reign of George II, that witchcraft ceased to be a capital offence. From then on witches became slightly more open in their dealings.

South-east Somerset continued to be the focal point for sorcery in England and numerous stories have been told of strange things happening here. Many a witch has been known, much wizardry has been experienced. But generally these witches have been tolerated, for they offered no real threat to their neighbours and gave no harm. A few were even welcomed, for they did some good.

In the mid 19th century the most famous witch of this area was Kitty Pitman. She lived at Milborne Port, in a little cottage next to the Newtown schoolhouse. There she looked after her mentally-retarded daughter Nan and generally kept herself to herself. She was harmless enough, it seems, but was prone to scaring her neighbours. She had the habit of gliding about the roads at night-time carrying her knobbled stick and one of her many black cats. Villagers were sometimes startled when she appeared in the dark, swooping down with her eyes ablaze. People shuddered as they passed her in the street, in case she cast a spell on them. At home, it was said, she had a cupboard full of books on the black arts, and these she would study and memorise. There is a story that one particular neighbour did upset her, and so received a curse in return. 'Thee hoss'll never goo to Yeovil again', she told him. And sure enough his horse died that very moment, falling down over the old woman's garden gate.

Another witch – this time a male witch – lived at South Petherton, west of Yeovil. In 1883 the *Pall Mall Gazette* reported a case of a local disturbance in the village of West Chinnock. Nine villagers, it seems, were summonsed to court accused of assaulting James Stacey, known in the district as 'the wizard of South Petherton'. They were part of an angry crowd of 140 which had chased the poor man through the village streets, kicking him, beating him over the head with sticks and throwing stones at him. He considered himself a herbalist, but the crowd called him a 'moonlighter', a 'vagrant necromancer' and a 'fortune-teller'.

An example of a 'white witch', who performed good rather than bad deeds, was Mrs Wills, who was known affectionately as 'Mother Hearn'. She lived during the early years of the 20th century in a little cottage high on the downlands above Milborne Port, on the Somerset-Dorset border. She was not so much a witch as a 'witch-doctor'. Her fame spread far and wide and over the course of some 20 years hundreds of people found their way to her door in search of cures, potions or just good advice. She was known to possess uncanny powers of magic – she grew and mixed herbs, she prepared medicines, she could foretell the future. She did not need to travel much, except for the occasional shopping expedition into Yeovil, since her clients came to her. People visited when they had illnesses that baffled doctors, or when they were anxious. During the Great War she was much sought by wives and girlfriends who were worried about their menfolk fighting in France. Rarely did Mother Hearn send people away disappointed. Sometimes she would treat a patient there and then with a 'magic' potion. Sometimes she would give a patient some medical advice – to someone with a swollen joint she might say, 'Go home and bathe it in water as hot as you can bear and bind it with bandages soaked in vinegar.' Sometimes she would merely say something like, 'Go home and the bleeding will cease by Wednesday, and the pain will depart.' Invariably her treatment, advice or forecast would prove correct. Indeed, she was a kindly soul. On one particular occasion a man went to her with financial problems, to ask her advice. She calmed his anxiety with soothing words, and then gave him £2 out of sympathy for his plight.

Witchcraft's Druid legacy makes a fascinating study for it brings to light the links between pagan rites, Christian practice and country folklore. In medieval Yeovil, for example, there was a Robin Hood celebratory fête held every year on Ascension Day. But Robin Hood, even in legend, never visited Somerset. The origin lay not in the stories of Sherwood Forest but in the tradition of earth reverence.

In Celtic times nature was worshipped. There were gods of rivers and trees, gods of wind, sun and sky. What we now dismiss as 'paganism' was in fact a pantheistic religion in which all living things were revered. Man was seen as part of nature's whole, all earth spirits being interdependent. But when Christianity spread, so this Celtic paganism was subsumed. Its gods were transformed into saints, its rituals into church practices, its festivals into Christian anniversaries – Brigid became St Bridget, water rites became baptism and Saturnalia became Christmas. The Celtic gods of whom the early Christians did not approve were turned into the Devil – Cernunnos, for instance, the horned god who was chief of the animals. Yet many of the old beliefs continued under the surface. Fairies, goblins and pixies remained the subject of superstition and tradition. And those who still held to these old philosophies came to be called 'witches'. Many witches even claimed that their mystical powers and knowledge had been acquired from 'the little people'.

Interestingly, the four annual witch gatherings, called 'Sabbats', coincided with the four seasonal celebrations of pagan times. Candlemas was linked to the Celtic festival of Imbolc, marking the start of the lambing season (31st January/ 1st February); Walpurgis was linked to Beltane, the Celtic spring festival (30th April/1st May); Lammas coincided with Lugnasa, the Celtic summer celebration of the harvest (31st July/1st August); Halloween was linked to Samhain, the peace-fire festival marking the end of the Celtic year (31st October/1st November). Our present May Day, of course, derives from Beltane, which celebrates fertility and growth. This pre-dates Lady Day. The maypole is an ancient pagan symbol and the dancing of young girls is symbolic of re-creation. The May Queen represents Mother Nature. In former times there was also the Green Man – Mother Nature's consort. Also known as Jack-in-the-Green and Jack-in-the-Bush, he was usually represented by a man dressed all in green, either in leaves and branches or else in green cloth.

As the Middle Ages progressed all the various strands of English tradition and superstition became entwined. Folk tales became mixed and country lore merged with country legend. In many parts of the country – as here in Somerset – the 'Green Man' turned into 'Robin Hood'. But it was not just the similarity of clothing that caused this particular transfer of identity, neither was it just the fact that they were both connected with forests.

In Somerset there is an ancient tradition of oak-men – tree spirits who looked after the oak woodlands. Usually these were seen as forest dwarfs, dressed in green leaves. Like Puck, they were mischievous goblins, half fairy and half human, who could change their shape at will. And also like Puck, they were thought to possess special magical powers.

In days gone by the alternative name for Puck, the merry wanderer of the night, was 'Robin Goodfellow'. The name 'Robin' thus became a country term for someone evil, mischievous or magical. It was from this origin that our wild flower, the ragged robin, was so named and, some say, it was also by this means that our favourite garden bird, the robin, was so christened. Originally this little creature was called simply 'redbreast'. But its mischievous nature led to the nickname 'Robin Redbreast', just as the wren was personalised as 'Jenny Wren'. But the nickname eventually superseded the real one and 'robin' became the bird's official name.

South-east Somerset, and especially the area around Wincanton, was once densely forested. Accordingly, it was cut off from other parts and remained relatively untainted by the cultural advance of the Saxons during the so-called Dark Ages. Many of the old Celtic, pagan, beliefs thus survived . As the Druids of Cadbury Castle had taught them, so many of the inhabitants continued to worship the ancient forest gods. One or two hypersensitive individuals, perhaps, even kept in contact with these gods, obtaining from them special magical skills. Such people were called witches and, in due course, were condemned and persecuted. But still they survived. It was not the Devil, however, to whom they pledged allegiance. When Elizabeth Style and Alice Duke were confessing their witchcraft to Robert Hunt, they spoke of a man dressed in black. But, they told the court, they did not address that man as the Devil. They always called him 'Robin'.

# 6

# TAUNTON AND THE BLOODY ASSIZES

The mystery of the ghosts of
Monmouth's rebellion, 1685

When the sun has set and darkness descends upon the cobbled courtyards of Taunton Castle, strange music can sometimes be heard. The beating of drums and the echoing tones of trumpets waft softly through the night-time air. And from the mullioned windows, through the leaded-light casements, flickering shadows may be seen. A candle burns – or is it a swaying lantern flame? Round the corner, at the Tudor Tavern, other strange sights and sounds may be witnessed – footsteps on the staircase and a creak on the banister rail. Some say that a mysterious apparition moves silently down the landing when the household lies asleep. Outside, in the streets and alleyways that stand over Taunton's old market place, the air is troubled. People say they have heard cries of pain when no one is about, screams of torture when all should be silent. Some even say they have smelt the stench of rotting flesh, carried in the wind on windless nights.

There are so many ghostly happenings in Taunton that few doubt their existence. For the town is still disturbed, its atmosphere still unsettled, by the memory of Judge Jeffreys and his Bloody Assizes, and the untrammelled brutality that went before. More than three centuries have passed since Monmouth's valiant warriors were brought here after their defeat at the battle of Sedgemoor. But still the town remembers. Generations have come and gone, and the world has moved on, but the scars persist.

Little of the original castle remains, but the part that does survive played a key role in the proceedings of 1685. It was the central portion, now housing the County Museum, that incorporated the Great Hall, where Judge Jeffreys held his court sittings. It was in this room, its walls draped with crimson curtains, that his Bloody Assizes took place, that his sentences were passed. And the Tudor Tavern in Fore Street was then a private residence owned by Sir William Portman. It was there that Judge Jeffreys was accommodated and entertained during his stay. In the old market place close by the gibbets were set up – it was there that the hangings took place. But it was not only hanging that went on. In many cases the bodies were cut down before death claimed them. Their limbs were hacked off and their bowels were plucked out. Sometimes the limbs were then dipped in boiling pitch and hung up on hooks, sometimes they would simply be thrown in the gutters for dogs to gnaw at. Heads were severed and stuck on top of poles; limbless bodies were set into iron cages and dangled from shopfronts where they would be left to rot. No wonder Taunton has never forgotten.

What led to this sad and sorry chapter in English history? What kind of men could inflict such torture on their fellow countrymen? What are the spirits that still disturb the streets and buildings of Taunton? And will their restless souls ever find eternal peace?

On the 11th June 1685 James Scott, the Duke of Monmouth, sailed into Lyme Regis harbour with 81 followers. His father, King Charles II, had died and he claimed the English throne. Most people thought he was one of the Merry Monarch's many illegitimate children and hence had no claim to the crown. But he and his supporters thought otherwise. They held that his mother, Lucy Walter, had been Charles' lawful wife – that a marriage ceremony had taken place which made him legitimate, and therefore the rightful heir. In addition, he was staunchly Protestant, as opposed to his uncle, James II, who was strictly Roman Catholic, and this also validated his claim. The people of the West Country evidently agreed with Monmouth's argument. Within days of his arrival 6,000 locals had rallied to his

*Taunton Castle.*

cause. His banner was raised and his march began.

For the next four weeks the Duke of Monmouth and his motley crew of rustics progressed through Somerset, gathering support. These weeks were called the 'Duking Days' and, for a while, Monmouth must have imagined that the tide of history was beginning to flow his way. All the Dissenters and Puritans of western England seemed to fall behind his banner. Some of the great families of the locality, like the Prideaux of Forde Abbey and the Plumleys of Locking Manor, offered support and everywhere the rebels were fêted and cheered. Progress through the countryside was quick. From Lyme Regis the growing army marched northwards through Axminster, Chard and Ilminster, reaching Taunton in just one week. On the 20th June, in Taunton's market place, Monmouth was proclaimed King. The cheers of the crowd could be heard in Creech St Michael. But the repercussions reached London. There the newly enthroned James II became alarmed. Accordingly, he sent troops westwards to crush the rebellion and capture the usurper. The war with the West Country had begun.

For the following fortnight Monmouth and his men toured Somerset, collecting supplies and recruits. For a while they were based in Bristol, then they moved on to Bridgwater. Meanwhile the King's troops marched down through Berkshire and Wiltshire to the Mendips, along the edge of which they skirted the Levels. On the night of the 5th July Monmouth's forces were camped just outside Bridgwater, and the King's forces were at Westonzoyland, three miles distant. The showdown was imminent.

There is no room here to describe in detail the sad story of the battle of Sedgemoor. It was a violent and bloody affair and the rebels had little chance against superior and better equipped fighting men. It was all over in a matter of hours.

Monmouth decided to attack and so led his gallant forces out of Bridgwater at about 11 pm, on the 5th July. The moon was full but the fog was up over the Levels, making visibility difficult. They circled eastwards, then southwards, to approach Westonzoyland from the Chedzoy direction. In the early hours of the 6th the command was given to charge. But Westonzoyland in those days was far more inaccessible than it is today. The Levels that stretched around it, called Sedgemoor, were dissected by many drainage ditches, known as rhynes. One of these ditches, called the Bussex Rhyne (which no longer exists), lay directly across the line of Monmouth's attacking forces. Unaware of its existence, the rebels soon found themselves having to wade across the cold, muddy waters of the channel. The result of the battle was never really in doubt. For many hours the brave but demoralised rebels struggled in the face of continuous gunshot. Those that reached the enemy lines were hacked to pieces. By dawn, Monmouth and his officers had fled the battlefield, leaving their followers to face the slaughter alone. More than 1,500 men were killed and about the same number were taken prisoner. Under 300 of the King's troops were killed. The 'Duking Days' were over.

Today the battlefield is marked by a simple monument – a block of Cornish granite with four hamstone corner pinnacles. A short inscription is carved and, sometimes, you will find a small bunch of flowers has been left in

*James Scott, Duke of Monmouth. (Somerset Archaeological and Natural History Society)*

remembrance. The place chosen for this memorial is close to a spot that was once a great mound, the site of a mass grave. It is said that, after the battle, not just the dead but the wounded also were flung into a large open pit. The bodies were stripped naked and left to rot. So many were the corpses that the pile built up to form a mound. Sand was subsequently thrown over the area, in an effort to stem the stench of decaying flesh. Today the mound has gone but the earth around continues to be sandy, a dry island in a peaty fen.

The Sedgemoor battlefield is still haunted, they say. At night-time a strange, eerie light hangs over the meadow, a green haze shimmering above the memorial stone. Phantom horsemen, with their cloaks billowing in the wind, are spotted riding across the marshes. Ghostly soldiers armed with pitchforks are seen charging over the rhynes. Not long past, a farmer was walking home late one night, skirting the field where the battle took place. He heard movement in the ditch – a splash in the water and a rustle of reeds. Then a voice called out, 'come over and fight'. The farmer thought it was merely a local drunk, who had fallen down the rhyne on his way home. But when he went to help, there was no one there. 'Come over and fight' – these were the brave but despairing cries of Monmouth's men as they stumbled their way to certain death.

The commander of the King's forces, initially, was Lord Feversham, a Frenchman by birth, who had taken full charge of operations. As a good Catholic he had little sympathy for the rebels and therefore showed scant mercy. Many of the wounded, taken at the battle, were allowed to die of their injuries, being left on the ground where they fell. Some 22 prisoners were hanged immediately, these being dangled in chains from the nearby trees. The royal troops were given total freedom, so they went on the rampage. When they reached Taunton the townsfolk hid in fear, while the shops were looted and the taverns wrecked. After a short while Feversham was recalled to London and awarded the Order of the Garter. But in his place arrived a man who was even worse, Colonel Percy Kirke. Kirke was notorious for his cruelty and rapacity, and his regiment – nicknamed 'The Lambs' – was already known to be the most vicious body of men in England.

The Lambs were so called because their regimental emblem was the paschal lamb, the Easter symbol, but their behaviour was anything but lamb-like. They terrorised Taunton with a ferocity that knew no bounds. For three months, until Judge Jeffreys was sent to implement the law, they ran amok. They set up camp just west of Taunton Castle, in a district later to be called 'Tangier' – after the fact that the Lambs had recently served in Tangiers, where they were fighting the Moors.

Kirke was in charge of this evil group of men and led by example. He imposed martial law, executing prisoners without trial and arresting anyone who dared question his authority. Upon first entering the town, he had 19 men hanged. Their bodies were cut up into little pieces and the bits were distributed around the streets as an example to the population.

For most of his time in Taunton, Kirke stayed at the White Hart Inn, which overlooked the market place. He used to like watching the executions from his balcony window, sometimes enjoying this 'entertainment' during interludes at dinner. Prisoners were generally hanged in batches of ten. He frequently ordered his military band to play whilst the victims swung from the gallows, their legs jerking in death throes. This, he said, was to give the condemned 'music for their dancing'. It is this macabre music that still wafts through the Taunton air occasionally, the drums and trumpets playing their ghostly and grisly tunes. Some of the victims were cut down from their nooses whilst still alive. They were then drawn and quartered, their wretched bodies being stretched and their limbs removed. Barrels of boiling pitch stood nearby and in these the severed flesh would be plunged. That August – the summer being especially warm that year – the stench must have been dreadful. It is said the aroma still lingers like a phantom pall.

One story recalls a young girl from Crewkerne who came to Kirke one day to plead for mercy on behalf of her fiancé, who was awaiting execution. She begged on her knees and wept for pity. Kirke promised that the young man's life would be spared if she consented to sleep with him and surrender, to him, her virginity. She reluctantly agreed. The following morning, in his bedroom at the White Hart, he led her to the window and drew back the curtains. There, dangling below, was the girl's fiancé, his lifeless body hanging from the inn sign.

Towards the end of September, Colonel Kirke was recalled to London, to answer charges. But it was not because of his barbarity that he was being summoned. It was because there had been rumours that he had been receiving bribes. Rich offenders, it was said, were escaping punishment by lining Kirke's pockets. King James needed to send someone else to Taunton.

George Jeffreys, born near Wrexham in Denbighshire and educated at Westminster School, had been Lord Chief Justice since 1683. By all accounts he was not a pleasant man. His debauched lifestyle had made him unhealthy and unattractive – his figure was swollen, his red face was bloated, his eyes bloodshot. He drank heavily and swore constantly. He smelt. He had a bullying, roaring voice and was prone to fits of uncontrollable temper.

Although he started his campaign of terror in August he did not reach Taunton until early October. The month of September was spent attending a series of trials in Hampshire and Dorset. At Winchester he had one old lady executed for treason, at Dorchester he had 29 unfortunates hanged on the flimsiest of evidence. He had been instructed by the King to show no mercy and was following these instructions assiduously.

It soon became clear that Jeffreys was intent only upon revenge. At Dorchester 300 prisoners taken at Sedgemoor awaited trial. Jeffreys promised mercy to all those who pleaded guilty. Accordingly most of them did plead guilty. They were hanged. Those to whom 'mercy' was shown were sentenced to transportation or severe whipping.

The trials that Jeffreys held – collectively known as the Bloody Assizes – took place at several West Country towns.

*Lord Chief Justice George Jeffreys. (Somerset County Council Library Service)*

At Exeter 21 prisoners awaited judgement, at Wells nearly 400 were being held. But it was at Taunton where most of the rebels were tried, so it was Taunton that bore the brunt of the terrible vengeance of the crown prosecution. The castle was still moated in those days and a drawbridge was used at the entrance. In total 526 prisoners appeared in the dock, some of these having been kept inside the castle itself, others having been brought from the notorious gaol at Ilchester. Many of those who had been cut about at the battle remained with their gashes undressed. Their clothes were filthy and bloodstained, their wounds festered. Day after day the corridors of the castle echoed with the tramp of feet as the soldiers marched the rebels to the court chamber; day after day wretched cries rang through the castle courtyards as the victims heard their sentences. The tramp of those feet and the cries of those rebels continue to sound within the castle walls. An army man is still sometimes seen on the first floor, a ghostly figure, booted and gauntleted, with a sword by his side and a pistol in his hand. Poltergeist manifestations are witnessed, even today, in the room now occupied by the County Museum and one curator has told of his experience of being clutched by a pair of ghostly hands.

No wonder Taunton Castle remains unsettled. In that fateful October of 1685, 144 men were sentenced to death, and many hundreds were sentenced to transportation. Those receiving the apparently lesser punishment were ordered to be sent to the West Indies, where conditions were notoriously harsh. Many were never to reach their destinations, the cramped conditions of the transportation ships offering a 30 per cent death rate from starvation and disease. Jeffreys once boasted that he had hanged more traitors than any of his predecessors since the Norman Conquest.

The hangings took place all over Somerset – at Ilminster, Wellington, Dunster, Chard. But it was those here at Taunton that were the most gruesome. The gibbets were set up in the market place, close to where Jeffreys himself was staying. A fire was constantly ablaze so that prisoners would see where their bowels would burn. All over the town, at crossroads, on the sides of cottages and over church entrances, relics of the punishments were displayed. The pitch-covered limbs and the flesh-ripped torsos were dangled from chains to swing in the breeze, and the severed heads were stuck on the tops of spikes to drip their grisly contents onto the horrified passers-by. All Somerset shuddered.

The ghosts of both Monmouth and Judge Jeffreys continue to be seen here in Somerset. On the Sedgemoor battlefield, some say, the Duke is still to be observed on cold, black nights, galloping his horse over the rhynes and into the darkness. And at many of the places where Monmouth stayed during the 'Duking Days', his ghostly likeness is said to stalk the buildings, at Sydenham Manor for instance and where Bridgwater Castle once stood. In Taunton Castle Judge Jeffreys continues to be seen from time to time, and also in certain places at Wells.

Yet both men died outside the county and were buried elsewhere. Or were they?

The accepted story is that the Duke of Monmouth escaped from Sedgemoor with a few companions. They travelled in secret for the next three days but grew increasingly tired, hungry and desperate. Eventually they were captured, the Duke himself being discovered lying in a shallow ditch in the New Forest, dressed as a poor shepherd, in an attempted disguise. Brought to London, he was subsequently committed for trial, accused of High Treason. Found guilty, he was beheaded on Tower Hill and buried in a nearby chapel.

But there is another story – that Monmouth did not die at the hands of the executioner. Many Somerset folk believed that the Duke remained hidden in the Polden Hills after the battle, and that a loyal officer sacrificed himself on the scaffold, impersonating his royal commander. Later, Monmouth was able to escape to Holland where he awaited the call. At a time when he was needed, he would return to Somerset. Did he eventually do so? Did he come back, in old age, to the county that gave him love and loyalty? We shall never know. But one of Monmouth's mistresses was taken to his body, as it lay in the coffin after the execution. She looked carefully, and searched in vain for the birthmark on his right arm. 'No', she said, ''tis not he.'

The story of the end of Judge Jeffreys is clouded in even greater mystery. Officially, Jeffreys was captured in 1688, soon after James II had fled from England. He was spotted in Wapping, disguised as a sailor, intending to escape by boat to Hamburg. Subsequently he was held in the Tower of London. There he wasted away. He died in 1689 and was buried in the Tower precincts. At a later date his body was removed to the Jeffreys' family vault in London's Cheapside.

But, here again, truth may be stranger than fiction. There is a story that Judge Jeffreys was actually buried here in Somerset. His sister Mary lived at Stocklinch, near Ilminster, and knew a man called Valentine Pyne, who held an official position at the Tower of London. In 1693, it is said, she bribed him to have her brother's body sent anonymously to Somerset, so she could give him a proper burial. But word got out and news spread that the unmarked coffin that arrived one night at Taunton contained the body of the hated judge. A mob broke into the chapel where it lay, prised open the coffin lid and decapitated the corpse. The headless body was then strung up in Taunton's market place. A few days later it vanished. Some generous-spirited locals had cut it down and conveyed it to Stocklinch, where it was finally laid to rest in St Mary's church, Ottersey, at the southern end of Stocklinch village. The tomb was unnamed, but when the coffin was discovered at a later date it was found to be much shorter than any other coffin.

Legend perhaps – but maybe not. Does the ghost of Judge Jeffreys still haunt the streets of Taunton because it is searching for its severed head?

# 7

# THE MAN WHO
# VANISHED

The mystery of a disappearance,
Shepton Mallet, 1768

It was a warm summer afternoon. The haymakers were in the fields and the good people of Board Cross, on the western side of Shepton Mallet, were going about their business. Owen Parfitt was sitting in his usual chair at the entrance to his cottage. He was to be found there most days, just outside the front door when the weather was fine, just inside when the weather was bad. He was a cripple and liked to sit there watching the world go by, chatting to his neighbours and joking with his friends. He was a popular old man and told a good story. He had lived a long and adventurous life and was fond of recounting his past exploits. Everyone knew old Parfitt. He was a local 'character'.

But on this particular afternoon – 6th June 1768 – events were to change from their normal routine. For Owen Parfitt was to vanish from the face of the earth – never to be seen again. His disappearance has been called 'one of the strangest unsolved mysteries, one of the oddest unexplained enigmas.' It has remained a puzzle to this day.

In fact, Owen Parfitt was, himself, a bit of a mystery. At this time he was about 70 years old, incapacitated and living with his sister Susannah. She was older than he was, and not in the best of health herself, but she managed somehow to see to his daily needs. In this she was helped by a young girl who lived opposite.

Brother and sister lived at Board Cross, in a three-storeyed cottage opposite the entrance to the turnpike road to Wells

– a thoroughfare now called Old Wells Road. Prior to his retirement and infirmity Owen had followed his old trade of tailoring. He had made and mended clothes for the Shepton Mallet inhabitants and had been well-known for his skilled craftsmanship. As a boy he had been apprenticed to a master tailor and had taken pride in the quality of his work ever since.

But the years between his boyhood as a tailor's apprentice and his settling in Shepton Mallet as an elderly man were shrouded in mystery. He told many stories of his past life but no one ever knew which of these to believe and which to ignore.

Certainly he had run off to sea at a young age to seek adventure. Some said he found his way into piracy, others said he had merely joined the merchant navy. Perhaps the truth lay somewhere between the two. Sea traders in the 18th century were not above a little bit of extra-curricular activity – some small-scale smuggling maybe or some profiteering in the wars that were going on at that time. In any case, America and Africa featured in many of the old man's tales and it seems likely that he really did have some acquaintance with those two parts of the world.

Susannah Snook, the young girl who helped Parfitt's sister look after the old man, gave evidence to the inquiry into his disappearance. She stated with some certainty that she had always supposed that Parfitt had joined the British Army when a young man. Could this also have been true? Possibly, since there is no reason why the young Owen might not have joined the army after finishing his life on the high seas. He was born in about the year 1700. This means that he might have gone to sea as a lad during the second decade of the 18th century and begun his army career some ten or twenty years later, in the 1720s or 1730s perhaps. This was a period of much British involvement abroad, with the War of the Spanish Succession and the expansion of the Empire. Britain's armed forces would have needed all the recruits they could get. In a long and exciting career there is no reason to think that Owen Parfitt could not have led two separate lives, first as a seafaring profiteer and then as an army adventurer.

*Board Cross today – the Parfitt home has now gone.*

Joanna Mills, a distant relative of Parfitt's, also gave evidence to the inquest. She said that she could not recall the old man ever having an army pension. But this does not negate his army career. Either Parfitt kept his personal finances private – in which case she would not have known about his pension anyway – or else he had not qualified for one. Army pensions in those days were not always given to everyone, they were often granted only to commissioned officers and to those wounded in action. Also, of course, a 'pension' sometimes took the form of a lump sum – a gratuity as opposed to a pension in the modern sense.

One mystery does remain, however, about Owen Parfitt's early life. When he settled down in Board Cross to live with his sister, it was generally known that Parfitt was a man of wealth, far more than a pension would provide. From where did he get all his money?

Sometime after his arrival in Shepton Mallet, Parfitt had suffered a stroke that left him partially paralysed. According to contemporary accounts, his subsequent movement was severely restricted. He could hobble a little and, when lying in bed, could manoeuvre himself around into more comfortable positions. But he could not easily move his arms.

Accordingly, he spent most of each day in bed. His sister Susannah fetched, carried and cooked for him and Susannah Snook from opposite came over to help when the old man needed moving. She was only 25 years of age and, according to some accounts, was distantly related to the Parfitts. Every afternoon it was the custom for the two women to carry Owen Parfitt from his downstairs bedroom, which was at the back of the house, to his favourite chair. This stood in the hallway. On pleasant days the old man would be deposited just outside the front door, the chair being placed on the pavement. On cold or wet days he would be put in the passage and the front door would be left open.

On the day in question – June 6th – the invalid's chair was positioned just outside the cottage entrance. There was still a slight chill in the early summer air, so the two women draped a large greatcoat over the old man's shoulders and a blanket over his knees. Underneath these, Parfitt still wore his sleeping garments. On his feet were soft bedroom slippers. Having made sure the old man was comfortable, the two women then went to make his bed and tidy his room. This done, sister Susannah went upstairs to tidy her own room whilst Miss Snook returned home, walking across the road.

A short while after – some 15 minutes according to her later evidence – Susannah Parfitt heard a noise. She was still upstairs at the time, in her bedroom, and the sound came from below. She went down to see if anything was amiss and found her brother's chair empty. Owen Parfitt had vanished. His greatcoat was still there, slung over the back of the chair, and his blanket was lying on the seat, but he himself had gone.

Immediately, the alarm was raised. Susannah Snook came over to help search the house, and other neighbours soon arrived to look in the local gardens. The haymakers in the fields nearby were asked if they had witnessed anything suspicious but they had seen and heard nothing untoward. More people then arrived – friends, relatives and the curious. Soon almost everyone in Shepton was taking part in the search. The town's population at that time was about 3,000, so everyone would have known old man Parfitt. What on earth could have happened? He could hardly have passed through the streets – on a busy summer afternoon – without being noticed. Besides, he was a cripple and could not have walked. And any other person – a stranger – who might have been carrying him would have been noticed as well.

The search continued into the evening. Groups of neighbours set out in different directions, to look in every street and alley, in every barn, field and ditch. Every wood and thicket was scoured; every pond, river and stream was dragged. All the wells in the town, all the caverns and caves, were investigated. But in vain. Owen Parfitt had vanished into thin air. The search continued through the night – despite a dreadful thunderstorm – but no sign was ever found of the old man, no clue was ever unearthed about his disappearance.

Susannah Parfitt was never the same again. She became silent, tearful and obsessed with the loss of her brother. She did not sleep for nights on end, but sat up waiting for his return. She grew morose and bitter. In due course she could not bear to be alone in that house ever again. She moved out of the cottage and took up residence with a friend nearby.

Rumours, theories, fanciful propositions, all kinds of stories circulated in the aftermath of Owen Parfitt's disappearance. Some said it was murder, others said it was suicide. Some people thought the old man had been spirited away by a supernatural agency, others said he had carried himself away by teleportation, using the spiritualistic powers of telekinesis. A few neighbours even pointed an accusing finger at the two Susannahs, suggesting that the women had schemed together to murder the old man and so inherit his fortune. One or two sceptics actually put forward the theory that Owen Parfitt had only pretended to be a cripple, and had made good his escape in order to prevent his relatives getting hold of his wealth.

In all these stories there were elements that may or may not be true, and it would be foolish to discount any of them totally. But certain facts do seem to point in one particular direction.

Shortly after Parfitt's disappearance, a neighbour recalled having seen an odd-looking man in the district. It appeared that this stranger was a seafarer, and had been asking questions about Parfitt's whereabouts. When, later, the old man was told that a seaman had been looking for him it is said that he turned ashen white and began to tremble. From then on he was sullen and thoughtful. A few days later Parfitt vanished. And the seafaring man was never again seen in the vicinity. Either Parfitt had made off with his money before anyone else arrived with a right to share it, or else the stranger himself carried Parfitt away. Yet in either case, it must still be asked, why did no one see anything amiss? Parfitt could have been disguised in some way, perhaps, but a stranger would still have been noticed.

The great thunderstorm that occurred within hours of Parfitt's disappearance led to a whole range of supernatural theories about the case. Somerset in the 18th century was an isolated, mysterious county, where folklore and legend played a powerful part in people's lives. Witches were feared and the Devil was believed to be ever present. Sorcery and magic flourished and anything that could not easily be explained through normal phenomena was put down to unearthly powers. It was remembered that Parfitt had visited Africa and America when young and it was thus supposed that he had mixed with mediums and sorcerers in those two continents. Those areas were thought to be inhabited by tribes steeped in the 'Black Arts'. Parfitt's knowledge of necromancy – so the theory went – had brought him into contact with the witches and wizards of Somerset once he had returned to England and moved to Shepton Mallet. In this way he had come to dabble in the supernatural sciences – an interest which led eventually to his weird departure from this life.

For the remaining years of the century the mystery rumbled on, with claim and counter-claim giving credence to one story after another. Then, at the beginning of the 19th century, a strange find reopened the case and some new theories arose.

In 1813 a certain Henry Strode inherited a house in Board Cross, only 100 yards from the old Parfitt cottage. He subsequently made some alterations to the property. During these human bones were dug up close to the garden wall. Upon further investigation an entire human skeleton was uncovered. At first people thought this might have been the remains of Owen Parfitt himself, but anatomical analysis revealed it to be the skeleton of a young woman. Who had she been? When had she vanished? At the time of Parfitt's disappearance a woman called Lockyer had lived at the cottage now owned by Strode. She had been a distant relative of Parfitt's and had been one of the many suspects linked to the old man's supposed death. Was the skeleton hers? A further mystery arose from the nature of the bones themselves. They revealed that the young girl, whoever she had been, had met with a violent death.

Such was the interest aroused by this find that, in the following year, William Maskell, the vicar of Shepton Mallet, acting as an attorney, decided to re-open the case. Many of the original residents were still alive (even though Parfitt had disappeared 46 years earlier) and there were still many different versions of the story circulating. Maskell thought that, by questioning those who could remember the facts, he could write down an authentic, definitive account.

Susannah Snook was still alive, now aged 71. She recalled the circumstances of the disappearance, how she had left Parfitt sitting in his chair and returned some 15 minutes later to find him gone. Another witness, Samuel Bartlett, had been 20 years old at the time and had known Parfitt well. He said the old man had been quiet, sober and generally happy. But a further witness, Joseph George, recalled how Parfitt had been prone to violent moods. Both agreed, however, that the old man had been a helpless cripple. Jehoshaphat Stone, yet another witness, was convinced that the mystery was entirely connected with the occult, saying 'Many folk round here at the time believed that Owen Parfitt had been spirited off by supernatural means.'

Maskell had, unwittingly, stirred up the neighbourhood once more and a plethora of fanciful stories swept the town.

The rumours started all over again. In 1820 an article in the *Western Daily Press* concocted an entirely new angle on the case, dismissing the supernatural theories and linking Parfitt instead to a sordid story of deceit, blackmail and intrigue. According to the article, Parfitt had settled down in Shepton with his ill-gotten gains. He went periodically to Bristol and returned, on each occasion, with a substantial amount of money. He never divulged the source of his wealth. He was, said the newspaper, a secretive, wicked old man with many strange tales to tell concerning the west coast of Southern Africa. He was a blackmailer of the lowest kind and had met his end when the blackmailed victim had at last silenced his tongue.

William Maskell's son, another William, continued to be interested in the case. In 1877 he published a descriptive pamphlet about the mystery, in which he recorded all the findings of his father's account, together with his own theories. He subscribed to the spiritualistic solutions, writing that 'the Devil had spirited away Owen Parfitt in the body'. In essence, he supported the supernatural idea of teleportation. According to Maskell junior, Parfitt was deeply unhappy. He hated being crippled and possessed a death wish. Using telepathic powers, learnt in his youth abroad, he thus spirited himself away using telekinesis, producing motion in the body without the application of material force. Such power is also possessed by fakirs and other holy men in the East, where levitation and transcendental movement are known phenomena. In Victorian England such powers were thought to be the work of the Devil.

In 1927 Dom Ethelbert Horne wrote about the Parfitt case in the *Downside Review*. In his article, a new theory was put forward. According to Horne, Parfitt was an unhappy man who decided to commit suicide whilst his two female carers were out of sight. He dragged himself to the nearest well, in the back garden, and threw himself down the shaft. He left his greatcoat behind to allow him to move more easily. The reason why his body was not subsequently found by the searchers, wrote Horne, was because it had been sucked sideways along a side tunnel. In those days all houses had their own water supplies, obtained from a garden well. When a well was being dug, water would be found at a certain known depth. If no water was reached at that depth, then a side tunnel – a horizontal shaft or 'drive' – would be cut, leading from the bottom of the well. In this way water would be reached and the well would fill up. If the Parfitt well had possessed a 'drive', argued Horne, then the body could have been pulled sideways with air pressure. The poles used by the searchers would thus not have discovered it.

Sadly for Dom Horne's theory, subsequent investigation found no trace of the body. In 1934 Charles Wainwright, a wealthy property owner who became intrigued by the Owen Parfitt mystery and studied all the relevant documents, had the garden well in question thoroughly searched. No human remains were discovered. So the mystery continued.

Did Owen Parfitt fake his own disappearance or was he murdered? Did he fall victim to a blackmailed criminal or a greedy member of his own family? Was there a serial killer on the loose in 18th-century Shepton Mallet, who listed both Owen Parfitt and a young girl amongst his victims? Was that mysterious girl, whose skeleton was found nearby, named Lockyer and thus one of Parfitt's relations? Was there anything supernatural in this case and, if so, what?

Arthur Conan Doyle, the creator of Sherlock Holmes and a dedicated believer in spiritualism, became fascinated by the Owen Parfitt case and wrote about it in the *Strand Magazine* in January 1920. He embroidered his account a little, but ended with these words, 'it is a freakish, insoluble borderline case and there we must leave it.'

# 8

# SPAXTON AND THE ABODE OF LOVE

The mystery of the vicars and the
virgins, 1846-1958

For more than 100 years, from 1846, the village of Spaxton, near Bridgwater, had some very mysterious inhabitants. They lived behind a high, stone wall on an estate which comprised several large houses, a church, a row of small cottages and spacious, landscaped gardens. Most of them were female and were called 'sisters'; a few were male and called 'brothers'. They were formed into a quasi-religious sect and their home was named the 'Agapemone' – a Greek word meaning 'the abode of love'.

And many were the rumours that spread out from this curious, hidden, secretive place. Many were the strange stories that emanated from this weird and wondrous site.

The sometime leaders of the Agapemone sect – the Reverend Henry James Prince and, later, the Reverend John Hugh Smyth-Pigott – had various titles, the 'Beloved', the 'Lamb of God', the 'Chosen', the 'Beloved One'. But how they controlled their followers, and kept their obedience, was something of a mystery. And what really went on behind those high perimeter walls? Some said that orgies were held, and even that rape was committed. Certainly there was evidence that illegitimate births had occurred. Glamorous young girls – virgins all – were seen to disappear through the front gates never to emerge. But there was never any trouble with the locals. All bills were settled promptly and the Spaxton villagers held the Agapemone in something approaching affection. There were no screams to be heard

83

and no one ever tried to escape. Indeed, members – the 'faithful' – appeared to come and go at will. They always seemed happy.

So what was the truth behind this Abode of Love? How was it set up and how did it survive for so long? What was life really like inside and who were the men that held such a powerful hold over the minds of so many apparently intelligent people?

It was all, in fact, the brainchild of Henry James Prince, onetime curate of the nearby church at Charlynch. And his story begins in Regency Bath.

Prince, the youngest of seven children, was born in 1811 at 5 Widcombe Crescent, Bath. His was not a rich family. His father died soon after his birth and his mother took in lodgers to help pay the bills. Young Henry was a frail, sickly child but very precocious. He was solitary by nature and soon became enthralled by the pious teachings of the Church. By the age of 12 he had learnt by heart the Scriptures – the Bible being his constant companion.

Evidently Prince had a personality of great magnetism and charisma. In his teens he became the subject of a mother-love fixation of a spinster who lodged at the house, a certain Martha Freeman. She became infatuated by the young man. She renounced her Roman Catholicism and fell under his spell. They spent long hours together, reading the Bible. Rumours spread about their relationship but no evidence was ever forthcoming that they had anything other than a purely platonic relationship. Martha may have been sexually frustrated but Prince, it appeared, was immune to the temptations of the flesh – at least, in his early years.

At the age of 16 Prince went to Wells to serve an apprenticeship with an apothecary, his mother wishing him to go into the medical profession. But this was not a great success. A few years later, therefore, he was sent up to London to study at Guy's Hospital. This was more successful. Prince proved an able student and passed his exams without much difficulty. He then returned to his home town and got a job at Bath General Hospital.

But Prince's heart was not really in his work, and he never

quite fitted into the profession that his mother had chosen for him. He had always wanted to go into the Church. So now, back in Bath, he renewed his close friendship with Martha and with her support – moral, spiritual and, indeed, financial – did what he had longed to do. In 1836 he abandoned medicine and went to St David's College, Lampeter, where he studied for holy orders.

It was at Lampeter that Prince began to develop as a forceful personality, fashioning his own brand of pious philosophy and evolving his own unique methods of religious argument. Some said he was mad. Others said he possessed demonic powers that could control human minds. A few simply thought he was especially gifted in the art of persuasion. From all accounts he certainly had charm. He also, evidently, had passion, together with a Svengali-like hold over those who fell under his mesmeric influence.

At Lampeter he formed a group of like-minded puritanical thinkers called the 'Lampeter Brethren'. This group held regular prayer meetings, produced religious tracts denouncing the 'debauchery' of the contemporary church, and generally behaved in a zealous, bigoted way. It interrupted religious services, gate-crashed college parties to stop 'ungodly drinking' and hounded those college lecturers whom it considered 'unworthy'. Prince was the unquestioned leader. He had, he said, developed a 'direct line' to the Almighty and no one doubted this assertion. As a student he was exemplary. He won numerous scholarships, became fluent in Greek and an expert on the Scriptures. Not surprisingly, he graduated with flying colours.

By the end of his course at Lampeter, Prince had established a power base. The Lampeter Brethren continued to thrive as a group and many of its devoted followers stayed faithful to their leader for the rest of their lives – becoming the mainstays of the Agapemone in later years. Prince had also established financial security – he had married the devoted Martha. She was the daughter of a sugar-planter in the West Indies and, as such, was a wealthy woman. As her husband, Prince could now draw upon her substantial annual income.

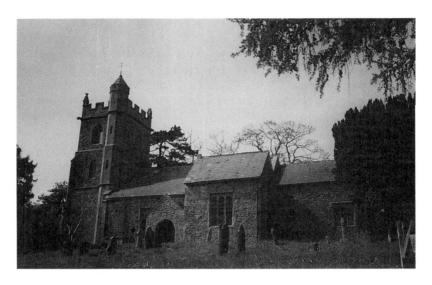

*Charlynch church – backdrop for some of Curate Henry Prince's seductive sermons.*

In 1840, having qualified, Prince was sent to Charlynch to become curate in a quiet Somerset backwater. There, so his tutors at St David's College had thought, this young firebrand could do little harm. How wrong they were! The parishioners at Charlynch were simple country folk and the rector (the Reverend Samuel Starky) was away most of the time, seeking rest cures on the Isle of Wight. He was something of a hypochondriac. Within just two years of Prince's arrival the parish was in uproar.

Using a style not dissimilar to that employed by American evangelists, Prince held mass religious meetings. Prayers were passionate, sermons were seductive, and congregations were held in thrall. Many members of the Lampeter Brethren turned up to give their support, and people came from far and wide to hear the wonderful oratory of the new young curate. Starky returned from the Isle of Wight and immediately fell under Prince's spell. He became a disciple to his own curate and joined the Lampeter Brethren.

By this time, it seems, Prince was beginning to think that

he really was the visible manifestation of God on earth. The Holy Ghost, he said, was moving him to convert the heathen. But the Charlynch Religious Revival was not like other religious revivals. Many of the meetings were held in secret and caused not a few tongues to wag. The Sunday school was re-established but no one was ever quite sure what the children were being taught behind closed doors. Certainly many a son and daughter returned home disturbed by the teachings. And the women's meetings were the subject of many a rumour. Wives and girl friends left their menfolk and went to swoon in the presence of their religious teacher. They would go to his private services, trembling for their souls, weeping with worries and distraught at their religious doubtings. Then – when the outer doors were closed – shrill voices would be heard, screams of passion and cries of joy renting the air. Later, they would return home, becalmed and happy, with gleaming eyes. The exact manner in which Prince had dispensed the grace of God was a secret shared only between him and them. What was this magnetism and power that Prince had over them?

But men were not immune from his brilliant oratory. Husbands, full of religious fervour, went home to beat their wives for their ungodly behaviour. Servants were sacked for not attending Prince's services, children were chastised for taking Prince's name in vain. The countryside, in short, was in turmoil.

After just two years at Charlynch, Prince had his licence to preach revoked by the Bishop of Bath and Wells. Effectively, he was expelled from the diocese. In his place the Reverend George Robinson Thomas was appointed. But since Thomas happened to be a member of the Lampeter Brethren, the revival continued, although not at quite such a pace.

Prince moved to Suffolk, where he became curate at Stoke, near Clare. By this time poor Martha had died and Prince had acquired, with indecent haste perhaps, a new wife. She was Julia, the middle-aged sister of Samuel Starky, rector of Charlynch. Julia was the wrong side of 40, but was rich. Prince's finances, therefore, remained secure.

At Stoke, Henry James Prince continued where he had left

off at Charlynch. Thunderous sermons were given, passionate prayers were said, secret meetings were held. Women swooned, men argued and children cried. The resulting uproar reached the ears of the Bishop of Ely, who summarily dismissed the new curate. After just one year in Suffolk, Prince found himself bereft of a living. How dare the Church of England expel him, the visible manifestation of the Holy Ghost! This proved the parting of the ways. Divine Guidance decreed that he, Prince, should take his Lampeter Brethren away from Anglicanism and set up his own church.

Accordingly, the 'faithful' were split into two groups. One went with Samuel Starky to Weymouth, where a house in Belfield Terrace was taken, to act as the centre for the sect; the other went with Prince to Brighton, where the Adullam Chapel became the focal point for conversions. And with the Lampeter Brethren went many new recruits gathered from both Charlynch and Stoke. Amongst these were the Nottidge sisters, five unmarried, middle-aged women, each in receipt of an annuity of £6,000 upon the death of their wealthy father. Women like these did not slip through Prince's fingers easily.

The sermons at the Adullam Chapel, with their heady mixture of hell, brimstone and damnation, had the followers flocking in. The Holy Ghost was coming and only their total subservience to Prince could save their souls. The house at Weymouth filled up and soon Prince himself, leaving Brighton behind, moved in to take charge.

The premises in Belfield Terrace evolved into the prototype of what later became the Agapemone at Spaxton. At this time Prince had not thought of the name 'Agapemone' but the idea of a formal religious sect revolving around his ideas and leadership began to take shape. He saw the advantages of running a community, on a single site, in which the 'faithful' could shield themselves from the outside world of 'unbelievers'. In such a community, he decided, sexual activity should be prohibited even amongst married couples. Husbands and wives would live separately and love would be spiritual only.

No longer was he preaching that the Holy Ghost was

coming. The Holy Ghost had come! He himself was the chosen one, he told his followers. No one disagreed. He set up a hierarchy of believers in his sect, running down from 'archangels' and 'angels' to 'brothers' and 'sisters'. These followers were promoted and demoted according to his whims, or, perhaps, according to their commitment to the cause. Generally, the followers were not from the poorest sections of society. As the rules became stricter and Prince's power became greater, so – interestingly – numbers rose. New members, and their money, flooded in. Soon the house in Belfield Terrace became too small. A larger establishment was required. Prince remembered his years at Charlynch and thought of the perfect site for his new venture.

During the summer of 1846 the Agapemone began to take shape. Some five acres were purchased at Four Marks, a crossroads hamlet east of Spaxton, close to the Lamb public house. On this site was built the complex that became the home of Prince's sect. There was a large main house with 18 bedrooms, numerous sitting rooms and servants' quarters, and in the grounds were a separate chapel, a row of cottages, and various stables, outbuildings and conservatories. The gardens were laid out with manicured lawns, gazebos and flowerbeds full of exotic plants. Around the perimeter was built a 15 ft high stone wall, pierced by gateways with studded oak doors. These defences, together with the bloodhounds that roamed the grounds, were intended to keep out inquisitive visitors, not to keep in the devoted faithful. Prince's followers were there willingly and could come and go as they pleased. Nearby, 200 acres of land were also purchased in the valley below Charlynch church, these being turned into an Agapemone farm, for the sect intended to be as self-sufficient as possible.

Money flowed in to finance these schemes. Sympathisers sent donations and many of the well-heeled members gave over their entire fortunes to the glory of the 'Beloved' – as Prince was increasingly being called. Titles and positions were awarded to the generous. A certain Hotham Maber, for example, who gave £10,000 to the cause, was created 'Angel of the Seventh Seal'. Three of the Nottidge sisters (Agnes,

*A contemporary view of the Agapemone or the Abode of Love at Spaxton. (Somerset County Council Library Service)*

Harriet and Clara) found their way to Spaxton, together with their collected wealth. They were rewarded with marriages to three of Prince's most stalwart followers in the Lampeter Brethren, George Thomas, Lewis Price and William Cobbe. Of course, these marriages were decreed by Prince to be spiritual only – they were not to be consummated (at least, not by the husbands).

90

By the end of the year the entire establishment was up and running. Although officially called the Agapemone, it became more commonly known by its English name – the Abode of Love. As 'The Lamb of God', Prince ruled over the proceedings with divine sovereignty. His word was law and his followers worshipped him. It has never been known whether or not Prince really believed his own philosophy. Did he actually think he was the 'chosen one' or was he an opportunist using his magnetic powers to charm and hoodwink innocent people? Whatever the answer, he cetainly seems to have created for himself heaven on earth.

Prince had given up his earlier abstinence and asceticism, now eating and drinking well and living in the lap of luxury. No expense was spared in the Agapemone's facilities. The furnishings were sumptuous, and the cellars were stocked with the finest wines. The chapel was decorated like a Victorian bar parlour. As well as the hassocks, hymn books and Gothic oak carvings, there were armchairs, side tables with periodicals scattered, draped curtains over the stained-glass windows, Persian rugs on the floors, and – in the centre – a large billiard table. Everywhere there were cushions embossed with a lion rampant on a bed of roses supported by a lamb and a dove, under which ran the inscription 'All Hail Holy Love'. A lion rampant, made of stone, was also fixed to the outside roof of the chapel, for this was Prince's personal emblem. Prince himself lived in the main house, in private apartments to which only the privileged few could gain admittance. One visitor later described his sitting room as resembling a lady's boudoir complete with lace curtains and delicate trinkets. Here Prince would sit resplendent in black frock coat and white cravat, speaking in a low, soft voice. Invariably his audience would consist of a number of beautiful young women, many of whom would be sitting at his feet in rapt devotion.

Life at the Agapemone was ordered and well-mannered. The number of people living there would average about 100 – in good times twice that could be accommodated, in lean times the number might fall to about 60. Members received no money or reward save for the 'honour' of serving their

*Part of the Agapemone as it appears today – most of the enclosing walls have now gone.*

master. The segregation of the sexes was enforced. The youngest and most attractive women – the 'selected ones' – lived in the main house; the older and less comely lived in the cottages, as did the menfolk. There was a strict hierarchy of privilege – members with money at the top, members without at the bottom. Long-standing followers of the Lampeter Brethren were the 'anointed ones' and held such offices as 'Keeper of the Seven Golden Candlesticks'. There were 'archangels' and 'angels' at the top of the pecking order, 'selected ones' and 'undefiled ones' further down, 'brothers' and 'sisters' further down still. Below these were those members who had not brought any wealth with them when they had joined. They were set to work as servants, becoming chambermaids, cooks, gardeners and stable hands. Selected from all the members were young, attractive women who were especially promoted to the positions of 'Brides of the Lamb'. We may guess about their particular duties.

Occasionally Prince would venture into the outside world with great pomp and ceremony. His excursions into

Bridgwater were preceded by an outrider, in liveried uniform, who called out 'Blessed is he who cometh in the name of the Lord'. Prince would then arrive in his carriage, surrounded by a heavenly host of young ladies. In 1851 he even travelled to London to visit the Great Exhibition. He caused quite a stir in Hyde Park, through which he was driven in an open carriage recently purchased from the royal family. The outriders blew trumpets and he was, as usual, accompanied by a bevy of alluring beauties. For a while he became the talk of the town. His sermons and pamphlets were widely read and his philosophy (such as it was) became fashionable. Back down in Somerset he began to receive letters addressed simply to 'Our Lord God, Spaxton'.

From time to time the Agapemone sect held large open-air meetings at which the Day of Judgement was proclaimed. These were well attended and much reported in the local press. But, inside the Agapemone, all was not strictly as virtuous as it might have been. The members kept the Sabbath only when it pleased them. They ate, drank, read and took strolls in the gardens. They undertook the tasks allotted to them by their leader and, when time permitted, went into the countryside. Carriage rides were taken over the Quantocks and shopping expeditions were made to Bristol and Bath. As for Prince himself, he certainly enjoyed the fruits of his labour. He had power, money, luxurious living and the devotion of beautiful women. He wrote the occasional hymn, poem or religious pamphlet, but, for the most part, he simply administered his mini-empire. He held special services and gave thanks to God – as well he might.

For over 50 years Prince's Agapemone prospered. Apart from one occasion, in 1856 when catastrophe struck, the years passed fairly uneventfully. Sometimes strangers would be seen coming and going, wealthy people from distant places, and sometimes a group of young women would be heard giggling in the grounds behind the walls, but the locals were tolerant. Traders had to deliver goods to a disembodied hand at the side entrance but all bills were paid promptly so what did they care what went on inside? Drinkers at the Lamb would gossip endlessly, and the rumours would become

*The chapel – scene of the 'Great Manifestation'.*

exaggerated, but their strange neighbours never caused any trouble.

The one time when adverse publicity really did damage the reputation of the Agapemone was in 1856. In that year Prince made the mistake of taking a 'Bride of the Lamb' in the presence of his entire membership. In what he later called 'The Great Manifestation' he summoned his flock to a special service in the chapel. During the singing and the chanting, it appears he passed amongst the most attractive young women in the congregation. Choosing one of these, he then led her to the altar. What took place there is not known for sure, but he spoke of 'taking the flesh of a virgin so that God's love could be extended from heaven to earth' – so we can but surmise. Of course, rumours spread like wildfire and cries of 'rape' rang out in the neighbourhood. The Sunday papers had a field day.

He was 45 at the time, and the girl was 16. Why he should take her in such a calculated and public way is a mystery. A few 'extra prayers' for the girl, held in his rooms, or 'additional instruction' after service might have achieved the

94

same end without the furore. It seems he was no stranger to seduction and could have chosen any number of methods of winning this particular prize. Perhaps he really did believe he was the 'Lamb of God'. Perhaps he really did think that a virgin had to be taken in the presence of the assembled gathering.

Be that as it may, the event undoubtedly damaged the image of the Agapemone for some years. Many members left in disgust – taking their fortunes with them – and Prince was forced to instigate a public relations exercise. Reporters were allowed in for interviews and pamphlets appeared that tried to justify the Agapemone's existence. For a while rumours became more extravagant and Prince was put on the defensive.

In truth, life within the Agapemone was probably less riotous and immoral than many people imagined. It was not a constant round of fun and games. There were no orgies with unfrocked clergymen frolicking with female 'saints', and there were no whipping parties or blasphemous, sacrificial ceremonies. Morals were strictly regulated – except, of course, those of Prince himself, who indulged incessantly with a succession of 'Brides'. Discipline was strict, food was ample and nourishing (rather than plentiful and exotic) and members generally amused themselves innocently. The place was not a prison, members being able to come and go at will. Prince had a number of illegitimate children – all remaining within the Agapemone to be educated – but none of the mothers ever complained or tried to leave. From time to time, outsiders brought lawsuits against Prince and his disciples for kidnapping and blasphemy, but these all failed. Prince broke no laws and caused no problems to the locals. The members were happy and did no one any harm.

In 1899, at the age of 88, Henry James Prince died unexpectedly. It was unexpected because his followers had imagined him to be immortal. His body was laid to rest in the gardens behind the Agapemone walls. A new leader had to be found, and in due course one was appointed, in the shape of John Hugh Smyth-Pigott. And he, evidently, was the man for the moment.

From all accounts Smyth-Pigott lacked Prince's personal charisma, but did have something of his magnetism. He was a good orator and possessed great business skill. Under him the Agapemone was to prosper and grow. And notwithstanding his own morals and sexual behaviour, the sect was to become more socially acceptable.

Smyth-Pigott, as a young man, had left the merchant navy to take holy orders at the London College of Divinity. After his ordination he had joined the Salvation Army, where he learnt many of his oratorical skills as a soapbox preacher. In this capacity he had impressed General Booth. With his fiery evangelism Smyth-Pigott was marked out as a man of destiny – he toured, lectured and, in his spare time, saved the souls of London prostitutes. In 1882, however, he left the Salvation Army to become an Anglican curate at St Jude's church in Mildmay Park, in London's East End. It was there that Smyth-Pigott first began to spread his wings as a man with a personal mission.

Like Prince before him, Pigott became a well-known and popular preacher, especially amongst female parishioners. His sermons were full of innuendo and sexual connotations, and there were many references to 'soul-brides' and the 'passion of the flesh'. He was a flamboyant exhibitionist and impressionable young ladies were seduced by his assertions of love. In due course he became too hot for the Anglican Church to handle, and he decided to go it alone.

It was probably during this period that Pigott first came into contact with Prince and the Agapemone. He travelled to Spaxton and liked what he found.

In 1896 Prince decided to extend his ministry to London. A new church was built on the edge of Clapton Common, in the East End, and this was given the name 'the Church of the Ark of the Covenant'. It was not long before Pigott was put in charge. It was a large, ornate church with turrets, a 155 ft spire and a massive oak hammerbeam roof. It was said to have a seating capacity of 1,000 – and Pigott was able to fill it.

At that time Pigott had a wife, Catherine – by all accounts a sweet, gentle, devoutly religious woman – but also kept several mistresses. At one point, it was rumoured, he had three concurrently, whom he called Faith, Hope and Charity. Later, by the time he went to Somerset, he had just the one, whom he named Sister Ruth. The list of Pigott's amours, over the succeeding years, could almost be a story in itself. Through his years at Spaxton he introduced a succession of female partners, called his 'soul-brides'. He did not believe in moderation. Once he claimed no fewer than seven soul-brides, one for each day of the week. As he grew older he became even more degenerate, and the number of soul-brides ran into double figures. His private apartments resembed a harem, his sexual appetite evidently being insatiable.

After the death of the 'Beloved' in 1899, it was only a matter of time before Pigott was officially proclaimed the new Messiah. The actual ceremony took place in 1902, when Pigott was enthroned at the Church of the Ark of the Covenant. On September 7th the pews filled with his devoted followers, who fell to their knees and wept for joy when it was announced that the Second Messiah had come. On the following Sunday 6,000 onlookers turned up, many to heckle and ridicule, many just out of curiosity. But the scene turned nasty and Pigott had to be protected by the local constabulary. Soon afterwards he moved to Spaxton, where he took up the running of the Agapemone. Thereafter the Clapton church remained empty for most of the time. It was well maintained, however, and all running expenses were met by the Somerset membership. Only occasionally did Pigott make an appearance there, to hold a special service or to interview prospective new members.

In Spaxton Pigott found the Agapemone in need of reform, as the farm and gardens had deteriorated and the membership had fallen. In addition, he found the sect had become isolated, cut off from village life and fossilised in Victorian conservatism. All this was to change under Pigott's powerful and skilled leadership.

Soon the organisation was moving with the times. Telephones, cars and electricity appeared and a successful membership drive led to an influx of funds. The farm was improved, the main house and cottages were renovated, the gardens were restocked. Unlike Prince, Pigott did not ignore the outside world but cultivated it. He gave interviews to reporters and arranged for the Agapemone to give large sums of money to local charities. Soon Pigott and his sect were pillars of the Somerset establishment – if not a respectable pillar then certainly an accepted and popular one.

Behind the walls of the Agapemone life became more ordered, and the community became more relaxed and friendly. The emotional, hot-house atmosphere that existed in Prince's day was replaced by a simple, almost monastic, ambience. Notwithstanding Pigott's own lifestyle, the 'faithful' kept to a rigid regime. Breakfast was taken at 8 am and consisted of porridge, tea, toast and jam. Prayers and hymns followed. Lunch at 1 pm was a simple two-course meal. Afternoons were spent at leisure pursuits – reading, walking, enjoying carriage rides and making shopping expeditions. Tea was taken at 4.30 pm (bread and butter, cakes and tea) and supper at 7 pm (soup, cold meats, cheese, tea and biscuits). Two special days were observed annually, Christmas Day and August 1st (Pigott's birthday). Members were allowed two weeks' holiday a year, when they could visit friends and relations. On a daily basis they were allowed to come and go as they pleased. Sexual intercourse was forbidden and segregated sleeping arrangements were maintained even for married couples.

Pigott himself, of course, did not keep to this strict lifestyle. His was an altogether more hedonistic existence. Whilst his wife Catherine lived in one of the estate cottages, Pigott took up residence in Prince's old apartments in the main house. There he was joined by Sister Ruth, by whom he fathered three children, christened Glory, Power and Life (two boys and a girl). By 1908 the total Agapemone membership was about 100, of whom 90 or so were female. These women varied in age, looks and wealth. The eldest and plainest lived in the cottages, the youngest and prettiest lived in the main house. It was from amongst the latter, of course, that Pigott selected his soul-brides. These were taught to love each other but, above all, to love the 'Beloved One'. They were told that

98

sexual intercourse was right only when it took place with Pigott – for then it represented the most sacred love of all. Thus, to become a 'Bride of the Lamb' was the highest privilege to enjoy. But these soul-brides were also taught the duty of secrecy, so that none dared to tell the others what went on behind closed doors. Each one believed she was the only soul-bride who had enjoyed Pigott's sexual favours, thinking the others enjoyed a purely spiritual love.

Pigott was nobody's fool and it says much for both his attractiveness and his powers of eloquent persuasion that he could hoodwink so many pretty and intelligent women for so long. It also says much for his cunning that all other members, living on the estate, seemed oblivious about what was going on in the main house.

For 25 years, under Pigott, the Agapemone flourished. Occasionally there would be a story in the newspapers – a soul-bride who left under a cloud perhaps, or maybe an illegitimate birth – but generally life continued amicably enough. The Great War came and went but membership remained buoyant. Indeed, so successful was Pigott in recruiting new members that, by the 1920s, he had even set up Agapemone cells abroad. In these miniature Abodes of Love, funds could be raised and potential soul-brides could be signed up. In Norway and France, especially, these cells prospered and exchange visits became a typical way in which the 'faithful' could take a holiday.

But time marched on and Pigott grew old. In 1927 he died, after a long illness. He was in his early 70s. The Agapemone was now left leaderless and on its own.

Douglas Hamilton, an elderly, dour Scot who had long been Pigott's deputy, took over the running of the Agapemone. But he was no new Messiah. He was a canny businessman, not a charismatic leader; he was a moral disciplinarian, not a pleasure-loving womaniser. He held the sect together – and indeed kept its finances healthy – but failed to inspire the faithful or enlist new members. By 1929 members had dwindled to just 37, of which 33 were women. One was a little girl and 3 were men (Hamilton himself and two gardeners). Life inside became glum, and the Agapemone grew to be a dreary place, with disillusioned elderly women and frustrated young ones. Catherine, Pigott's widow, kept the charity work going for a while, taking hampers to the sick and alms to the poor, but she died in 1936 at the age of 85. She was truly loved by the locals and sorely missed. Six years later Hamilton himself died. He was also in his 80s. Leadership then passed to Sister Mary, who had lived at the Agapemone for 40 years, and Sister Ruth, mother of Pigott's three children. The latter died in 1956, aged 90. Soon afterwards the Agapemone closed altogether and the few remaining members dispersed. At auction in 1958 the entire site was sold to a developer, who subsequently divided many of the buildings into flats.

Today the onetime Abode of Love is a sad sight indeed. The church has been desecrated and is the subject of constant repair. The main house is owned by someone who runs a breaker's yard and old motor cars are parked in the gardens. Some of the buildings at the back are in better shape and an old people's home now occupies much of the site.

But many of the Spaxton villagers still remember the last days of the sect. In the Lamb a plan of the original Agapemone can be seen, showing the ground and first floor distribution of the rooms. Sometimes a customer may come in and ask about the history of the place, having read something of its strange story. In 1985 Patrick – otherwise known as 'Power' – Pigott died, thus ending the last connection with the Second Messiah. One or two of the more elderly residents have fond memories of Ruth and the other last surviving 'sisters'. They were kindly women who did many good deeds.

And what of the Agapemone reputation? Prince and Smyth-Pigott were regarded by many as monstrous, evil, depraved charlatans. Perhaps they were. But no one was ever dragged to the Abode of Love unwillingly, no one was kept behind its walls forcibly. No crime was ever committed and some good was done. A few local charities benefited and the lives of many people were improved. The 'faithful' were generally happy. Some of those women living at the Agapemone might otherwise have led sad, pointless existences – in soulless jobs perhaps, or as the drudges of loveless marriages. At least the Abode gave them food, shelter, companionship and a philosophy which provided a purpose to life.

As for Prince and Smyth-Pigott, they successfully created for themselves an earthly paradise. To what extent they really believed their own religious claims – their godliness, righteousness and infallibility – we may never know. But their followers seemed to have no doubts. They accepted totally that the Agapemone gave them a passport to paradise. There is a story, still circulating in Spaxton, that those of the 'faithful' who died behind the walls were buried in the gardens in a standing position – to ensure their speedy transfer to heaven. This particular mystery remains to be solved.

# 9

# THE 'LOST' CHAPELS
# OF GLASTONBURY

### The mystery of discoveries made by
### psychic research, 1907-22

Glastonbury is unique. It is the ancient centre for both Christian and pagan beliefs, and the natural crucible where a myriad of cultural and psychological experiences coalesce. There are strange forces at work here – mystical phenomena that cannot easily be explained through any cold, scientific experiment. There are mysteries here that remain unsolved, theories that remain unproved.

In 1907, on the 7th November, two men sat down at a desk in a room overshadowed by Glastonbury Tor. One was Frederick Bligh Bond, the other was John Alleyne. They were alone. Alleyne held a pencil over a blank sheet of foolscap paper, Bond held his right hand lightly on the back of Alleyne's so that his fingers lay evenly across the surface. Bond then spoke out aloud, asking the question 'Can you tell us anything about Glastonbury?' Slowly Alleyne's fingers began to move, driven by an unknown force, and small, irregular writing began to appear on the paper. The words were roughly scrawled, but they could just be deciphered. They read, 'All Knowledge is Eternal and is Available to Mental Sympathy'.

Then, as Alleyne's fingers continued to move across the paper, a scribbled diagram appeared. It was an outline of the abbey church. Down the middle of this plan a name was then written, 'GULIELMUS MONACHUS' – William the Monk.

And so began a most curious sequence of events. Bond and Alleyne continued to explore their new discovery – that the

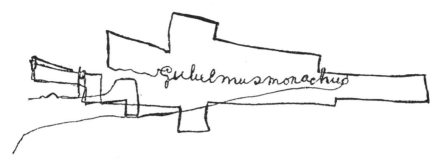

*An example of a diagram of the abbey produced by automatic writing, showing the 'signature' of William the Monk, and originally reproduced in Bond's book* The Gate of Remembrance. *(With acknowledgements to Blackwell Publishers)*

strange phenomenon of 'automatic writing' would help them in their research.

Frederick Bligh Bond, a well-known architect and restorer of old churches, was a member of the Somerset Archaeological Society. John Alleyne, a colleague, was an associate member of the Society for Psychical Research. Together they were investigating the archaeological remains of Glastonbury Abbey, and were embarked on a project to map the entire site of this once great monastery.

In anticipation of his appointment as Curator, and Director of Excavations at Glastonbury Abbey (an appointment confirmed by the Church of England trustees in 1908), Bond devoted much of 1907 to an initial study of the ruins. He was aware that his friend Alleyne possessed the power of automatic writing, and thought this method of psychic research might help him answer certain questions that old documents and current archaeological evidence had failed to solve. Where, for example, were the Edgar and Loretto Chapels exactly located? He knew they had existed – they were built during the early 16th century – but did not know precisely where to find them. The existing information gave few clues.

What the two men were eventually to discover was both fascinating and explosive. The world of archaeological research was never to be the same again, and Glastonbury

103

*The abbey ruins, with the remains of the Edgar Chapel in the foreground.*

was to acquire one more inexplicable mystery.

So what exactly was this psychic power – this automatic writing – that Bond and Alleyne had harnessed? What were the discoveries made by these two men using this particular method of research and what was the response of the archaeological and ecclesiastical establishments? When will other examples of psychic research be recognised? And why does Glastonbury produce so many mysteries, of which this is just one example?

The town of Glastonbury, with its ancient abbey, its holy wells and its wondrous Tor, has long been at the heart of religious mysticism. From its Celtic origins as a sacred site, pagan then Christian, it grew steadily in importance through Saxon times, first as a military stronghold then as a monastic and cultural centre. Apart from being the legendary location of Avalon, it also claimed direct links with Christ through the story of Joseph of Arimathea. The chalice used at the Last Supper – King Arthur's Holy Grail – is said to be buried hereabouts and the Holy Thorn traditionally still flowers at Christmastide. The earth's energies, too, are supposedly concentrated here – ley lines meet and the forces of cosmic symbolism are enlightened by the subtle shapes of the living landscape. The 'Glastonbury Zodiac' and the 'Glastonbury Maze' are visual proclamations of this spiritual power – foretelling, perhaps, the coming of a New Jerusalem. With such a concentration of cultural and historic tradition, of legend and myth, of spiritualism and astronomical conjunction, it is little wonder that the science of automatic writing should have been experienced here as well. Frederick Bligh Bond and John Alleyne maybe did no more than make contact with the existing forces that are forever swirling about this most mysterious of places.

To the Celts, Glastonbury was Ineswytrin – the Island of Glass. There was a pagan temple here until the time of Christ, when it subsequently became the location for one of the earliest monasteries in England, being founded by the first Christian monks arriving from Ireland. Later, under Ine, the Saxon King of Wessex during the 7th century AD, the monastery was re-established. Growth in both size and power then continued apace. Dunstan became Abbot in AD 940 and it was from here that this saintly man began his Benedictine reform of the English Church. By the time of the Norman Conquest, Glastonbury had been developed into a major centre for pilgrimage. Not only were the Saxon kings interred here, but also the saints Aidan and Paulinus.

King Arthur is also said to have been buried at Glastonbury. In the 12th century – at about the time of a great fire that destroyed the abbey buildings – the monks discovered the bones of a tall man. Upon the coffin were the words 'HIC IACET SEPULTUS INCLYTUS REX ARTURIUS IN INSULA AVALONIA' – Here lies buried the famous King Arthur on the Isle of Avalon. Whether or not this find was honestly made, the link between Glastonbury and the Isle of Avalon was undoubtedly convincing. The name Avalon derived from the Celtic for 'Island of Apples' and Glastonbury was indeed an island where apples were grown, what are now the Somerset Levels being an area of marsh and watery inlets. If Arthur did ever exist he would have been a Romano-British chieftain who organised a resistance movement against the invading Saxons. The legendary battle of Camlann, at which Arthur was killed, may well have a basis in fact. Glastonbury was one of many Celtic fortresses dotted around the West Country and several major battles did take place in what is now Somerset.

Indeed, Glastonbury was especially important in Roman-British times. Not only did it act as a military and religious capital, it also grew as an important trading centre. It is said that in AD 63 Christ's uncle Joseph of Arimathea came here, partly to trade in tin and iron ore (both mined in the West Country) and partly to help the native monks convert the Britons to Christianity. The story is told how he landed by boat on the side of Wearyall Hill and thrust his staff into the grassy slope. The staff took root and grew into a thorn bush, to blossom each Christmas. Joseph also brought with him the cup that had been used by Christ at the Last Supper. That cup is now said to be concealed somewhere beneath Chalice Well – hidden since the time of Arthur's quest, when it was more commonly called the Holy Grail. The little chapel built by Joseph, made of wattle and daub, was used to baptise the first British converts. It later formed the focal point for St Patrick's monastic community, on whose site now stands the Lady Chapel and the western end of the abbey church nave. Whether or not Christ ever came to Glastonbury is of course a matter of great controversy – and is discussed in William Blake's well-known words 'And did those feet...', which became the hymn *Jerusalem*.

There is a body of opinion that says that the Age of the New Jerusalem will soon be upon us. The 'Glastonbury Zodiac' and the 'Glastonbury Maze' bear witness to a paradise to come. Both are best seen from the air. The 'Zodiac' is an interlocking pattern of curves and shapes whereby the astronomic symbols are marked out in the landscape around the town of Glastonbury, hillslopes, ancient trackways and rivers forming the figurine outlines. The Tor itself forms Aquarius. The 'Maze' is a labyrinth of grassy undulations cut into the slopes below St Michael's Tower. Far from being mere sheep tracks, it is said, these indentations were carved by ancient peoples to harness earth forces and help

THE 'LOST' CHAPELS OF GLASTONBURY

implement the miasmic energies of both past and future. Meanwhile, the wider findings of Geomancy and Gematria – ancient sciences which recognised that the living landscape has arrangements and patterns possessing mystical and mathematical regularities – further enhance the subtle yet awe-inspiring phenomena at work in this part of Somerset.

Frederick Bligh Bond and John Alleyne were evidently in tune with these all-powerful energies, and subconsciously responded to their mystical envelopment. When they sat down on that fateful November afternoon in 1907 they inadvertently made contact with the vibrant magic that permeates the Glastonbury air. They channelled the psychic powers of automatic writing to rekindle the strange forces of 'universal memory'.

Bond described automatic writing or 'automatism' as that branch of psychic research which harnesses the ability within certain people to tap into the 'Great Memory' that pervades the individual in history. Every single person, he said, possesses a transcendental consciousness. Within each mind there is a door through which Reality may enter. This Reality derives from a cosmic Memory which embraces both individual experience and the experiences of others past and present.

This may sound complicated but the theory is, in fact, simple to explain. It argues that the knowledge acquired by all individuals, both separately and collectively, does not die with them. Instead it remains behind to form a kind of Universal Knowledge. This is kept in everyone's subconscious. Those people with the power to 'plug in' to this Universal Knowledge can repeat the information of past ages, even though they may not, personally, have acquired it. John Alleyne possessed such powers. When sitting at his desk, pen in hand, and with spiritual concentration, he could contact the minds that held past knowledge. The medieval monks of Glastonbury became the agents of these powers and through automatism directed Alleyne's pen.

The idea that there exists a 'Great Memory' or 'Universal Knowledge' was not new in Bond's day and many scientists and psychologists since then have expounded views that complement the same theory.

People have even suggested that the power of automatism is implied in the Bible. Foretold by Isaiah, the extraordinary 'gift of tongues' was demonstrated by the concourse assembled in Jerusalem at Pentecost. St Paul, in his first Epistle to the Corinthians, links this gift to religious inspiration. When believers gathered together and 'spoke in tongues' they all appeared to understand the message, even though the speakers knew little or nothing of the actual sounds they made. Could it have been that the sounds and words were being transmitted by others, through the Universal Knowledge? The gift of tongues was sadly abused in the Church at Corinth and the power was subsequently withdrawn 'in the wisdom of God'. Today certain charismatic Christian groups, like the Pentecostalists, still practise this 'gift of tongues' and perhaps these too are connecting with the Great Memory. Automatic writing can thus be viewed as the written equivalent of 'speaking in tongues'.

The early 20th century saw much research into the human mind and many philosophers have identified phenomena not unlike those suggested by Bond. For example, C.G. Jung developed the theory of the 'collective unconscious' and W.B. Yeats propounded the ideas of 'anima mundi' and 'spiritus mundi'. In more recent years Rupert Sheldrake has proposed the theory of 'morphic resonance'.

Carl Gustav Jung (1875-1961) was a Swiss psychologist and psychiatrist whose work profoundly influenced the course of theological study. Apart from the development of analytic psychology, he suggested that ancient alchemists constructed a kind of textbook of the collective unconscious which subsequently became held and shared by everyone. Thus, he explained, the strange experiences that people have, in their dreams and fantasies, often contain elements and symbols commonly found in old alchemy. Thus, modern dreams could feed off a common knowledge and experience.

William Butler Yeats (1865-1939) the Irish poet, critic and dramatist, had a similar theory but expressed it differently. He linked imagination, history and the occult and said that they co-existed. Hidden Ireland, for example, he said, was largely a product of its customs, beliefs and holy places. History was cyclical with a recurrence and convergence of images, so that they became multiplied and enriched. With the twin concepts of 'anima mundi' and 'spiritus mundi', there were natural and spiritual images that existed beneath consciousness. Certain individuals could break through the barriers of time and space, and tap these universal truths.

In recent years Rupert Sheldrake, the scientist who continues to study the world of unexplained psychic and physiological phenomena, has proposed certain additions to the ideas of Jung and Yeats. In his theory of 'morphic resonance' he suggests that plant, animal and human life have an inherent memory, so that life forms can recreate behaviour acquired from former life forms. Individual memory and the capacity of learning, he says, takes place against a background of collective memory. This memory is inherited from previous members of the same species.

So Frederick Bligh Bond and John Alleyne were not alone in their belief in automatism, and the years since their collaboration have seen further advances in their philosophical ideas. It could be argued that, far from being misguided, they were actually ahead of their time.

In 1907, when Bond and Alleyne began their psychic research, with the object of investigating the abbey's ruins, not much was known about the Edgar Chapel. Historians knew when it was built, but there was doubt about its exact location. After his visit in 1533 – six years before the abbey's dissolution – John Leland wrote in his *Itinerary*, 'Abbate Beere builded Edgares Chapel at the Est End of the Chirch'. But the impression given by this statement – that the chapel stood beyond the altar, at the far end of the choir – had been questioned by some experts. James Parker, for instance, suggested in 1880 that it stood in the south transept, to the east of the nave. The exact size of the Edgar Chapel was also unknown and archaeologists varied in their opinions. Some said it was a small side chapel, others said it was more substantial, being similar to St George's Chapel at Windsor Castle or Henry VII's Chapel at Westminster Abbey. What everyone did agree upon, however, was the chapel's great beauty – old accounts speak of delicate stonemanship.

The Edgar Chapel was amongst the last buildings to be constructed at Glastonbury Abbey and must have been newly finished when Leland visited. It was begun by Richard Beere who was Abbot here from 1493 to 1524. As part of a general enlargement – Beere also added the crypt under the Lady Chapel, two side chapels and the vaulting under the central tower – the Edgar Chapel became the crowning glory of the abbey church. It was dedicated to the first King of all England, who was crowned at Bath in AD 973, and contained some of the most intricate tracery and sculpture then to be known.

From all accounts the Edgar Chapel survived the initial destruction of the Dissolution of the Monasteries and was still standing at the beginning of Elizabeth I's reign. Demolition came later, the exact time is not known. It had certainly disappeared by the early 18th century, when William Stukeley, the antiquarian, visited Glastonbury.

So Bond and Alleyne had a lot of information still to uncover when they began their strange search into the Great Memory. They were not to be disappointed.

Between 7th November and 30th December 1907, nine separate sittings were held. In each case Alleyne's hand was

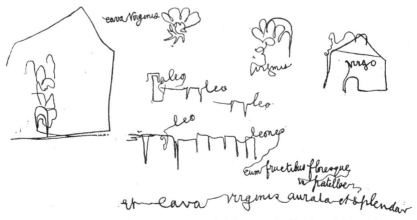

*Further examples of the 'automatism'. The words 'leo' and 'virgo' were taken to indicate statues of Lions and the Virgin on copings and exterior walls. (With acknowledgements to Blackwell Publishers)*

guided by the irregular pressure of a mysterious force. There were diagrams, technical architectural data and long descriptions of medieval Somerset. These writings, it appeared, were derived from different sources – 'Rolf Monachus' (Rolf the Monk) and 'Johannes de Glaston', for example – but all had similarities suggestive of a common origin. The sentences were in Saxon English and rough Latin – languages commonly used by medieval monks but little known to Alleyne – and the sketches were rudimentary. The messages were freely scribbled, but all the writings were decipherable and made sense. And what they told Bond and Alleyne was fascinating. Apart from general information about Glastonbury Abbey in the Middle Ages, and about the life of Johannes de Glaston, later identified as Johannes Bryant, a Glastonbury monk who had died in 1533, there were such architectural details as the site, size and character of the Edgar Chapel. Specific dimensions were given.

Bond and Alleyne were not, actually, sure whether they had contacted a group of monks, congregated together and thus indicating a large field of cosmic memory, or else a succession of different monks, representing separate small fields of cosmic memory. But what they were certain about was the reality, dedication and commitment of the power into which they had been transported.

During the first nine sittings the two men were told many and various facts about the Edgar Chapel. For example, that it was about 30 ft wide and 70 ft long, had an entrance door behind the reredos, five paces wide, and was polygonal at its eastern end. None of these facts were known by historians at that time but they were all proved by subsequent excavations, undertaken a short while afterwards and supervised by Bond.

The window glass was azure, according to Johannes, yet historians had always thought gold and white glass were more common in 16th-century buildings. But, later, archaeologists found blue fragments of glass in the dug-out trenches, so confirming the monks' information.

Bond and Alleyne continued to hold sittings throughout 1908 – another 30 in fact. Most of these were still in contact with Johannes but other monks also appeared, including 'Reginaldus' and 'Robert'. This time information was given about the little crypt under the stairs of the Edgar Chapel, the gold and crimson ceiling and the triple arcade behind the altar. Once again, none of this detail was known by historians at the time but was later confirmed by excavation. More precise dimensions were also provided, allowing Bond to make an exact plan of the entire Edgar Chapel as it had stood at the time of the Dissolution. As before, later archaeological evidence proved the accuracy of the writings. Bond and Alleyne kept detailed notes, forming a complete record of this remarkable tale of discovery. But their research was met only with disbelief and scepticism from the archaeological and church establishments.

Encouraged by their success over the Edgar Chapel, however, Bond and Alleyne turned their attention to the other 'lost' chapel – the Loretto. This time their sittings took place during two separate periods – in 1911 and 1917. During the first period they received messages from Abbot Beere himself, and during the second they were in contact with the spirit of 'Camillus Thesiger', otherwise known as Camel, the purse-bearer to Abbot Beere, whose marble tomb lies in St John's church.

In the years 1503 and 1504 Abbot Richard Beere made two trips to Italy. During the first visit he was to negotiate, on behalf of the Crown, a papal dispensation for Catherine of Aragon to marry her brother-in-law Henry, Prince of Wales (later Henry VIII). During the second visit he was to deliver the Order of the Garter to the Duke of Urbino. It was during this second visit that Beere became deeply impressed by the shrine to Our Lady of Loretto. According to legend, the Holy House (Christ's home in Nazareth) was miraculously transported through the heavens to land intact in northern Italy. Upon his return to England Beere proceeded to build an elaborate chapel at Glastonbury, dedicated to Our Lady of Loretto – such was his enthusiasm for Italy.

As with the Edgar Chapel, historians and archaeologists could not agree about the exact location of this Italianate chapel. It was destroyed with the rest of the abbey in Tudor times and little evidence remained. John Leland merely described it as 'joining the north side of the body of the Church'. William Stukeley did not mention it in his *Itinerary* of 1723. Some archaeologists thought it was a large, detached building, others considered it was merely an internal structure within the north transept.

The scripts produced by the 1911 and 1917 sittings, taken together, were comprehensive and Bond was able to draw a fairly accurate plan showing the exact position and size of the chapel. According to these scripts there was a vestibule, or 'claustria', adjoined to the west wall of the north transept. This led to a separate chapel, which had the dimensions of about 40 ft by 20 ft.

Again, Bond's information – as given through automatic writing – was met with scepticism from the ecclesiastical authorities. But, once more, it was Bond himself who was to be proved right. During excavations in 1919 and 1920, stone foundations were discovered west of the north transept. And there, as forecast by the automatic scripts, was the outline of the Loretto Chapel.

Between the years 1908-1922 Bond discovered a wealth of further information. He located the two western towers, the great north porch, the shape of the transepts and much of the layout of the monastic buildings south of the abbey church. He published his discoveries in the *Proceedings of the Somerset Archaeological and Natural Historical Society*, and in 1909 wrote the much respected book *An Architectural Handbook of Glastonbury Abbey*.

In spite of all this, Bond's discovery of the Edgar and Loretto Chapels, using automatism, failed to impress the authorities. In 1918 he published *The Gate of Remembrance*, in which he described in detail the story of his discoveries. But this only brought him ridicule. The orthodox establishment was sceptical. The Dean of Wells, Joseph Armitage Robinson – who was also a writer and historian – was said to have been 'appalled' by Bond's investigations. Some archaeologists dismissed automatism altogether, saying that Bond had access to 'unknown manuscripts'. But no one ever produced any evidence to support this accusation.

113

*A scale model of the abbey showing the two lost chapels.*

The relationship between Bond and his Church of England employers deteriorated to the point that in 1922 he was dismissed from his position. He later left England, a broken man, to live in America. He died in 1945. As for Alleyne – he disappeared from the public gaze. The exact relationship between Bond and Alleyne, and the reasons that might have led to their strange supernatural skills, were to remain a mystery.

Today the ground plans, drawn in the Glastonbury Abbey guidebooks, show the position of the Edgar Chapel but do not indicate the apse at its eastern end. Neither do they show the position of the Loretto Chapel – although a model in the entrance display does. Both the Edgar and Loretto Chapels are mentioned in the guidebook texts but the work of Bond and Alleyne in their discovery is omitted. Why?

Automatism, it is true, can be seen as a curious science. But total rejection by official bodies is surely not the way to respond to this particular form of research. Perhaps the church authorities should recognise that Glastonbury is more than just a Christian site, and that the true mysteries found here are much stranger than anyone can imagine even now.

# THE BODY ON THE KITCHEN FLOOR

The mystery of the Baltonsborough
murder, 1937

It was Wednesday, 9th June 1937. The jury had returned to
the court after just 20 minutes of deliberation. The verdict
was then announced. William Samuel Rendell was guilty. Mr
Justice Lawrence placed the black cap upon his head and
pronounced the sentence of death. The convicted man was
led away to the cells to await execution. Some little time later
he was hanged.

In some ways it all seemed such an open and shut case.
William Rendell, an itinerant farm labourer, had murdered his
wife, Lily. Her throat had been cut from ear to ear and her
head beaten in with a chopper. He had confessed and made
a full statement to the police. The evidence was clear and the
verdict was delivered to an expectant public.

But was the verdict justified? Was some vital evidence
withheld that might have made the jury come to a different
conclusion? Did William Rendell really kill his wife or was he
prepared to die in order to protect someone else?

These questions have never fully been answered, and so
the Baltonsborough murder remains a mystery to this day.

Just a few miles south-east of Glastonbury, Baltonsborough
is not the kind of village one would usually associate with a
violent murder. It is quiet and picturesque, friendly and
undisturbed by the worst excesses of 20th-century
development. Standing in the midst of the Somerset Levels,
on the banks of the river Brue, it consists of a huddle of stone
cottages, nestling around a medieval church. In summer

*Kite Lane, Baltonsborough – the Rendells' cottage once formed part of this building.*

months the little lanes are alive with flowers. Baltonsborough's one claim to fame is that it was the birthplace, in AD 924, of St Dunstan. This kind, well-mannered and accomplished man first rose to prominence when King Edmund appointed him Abbot of Glastonbury. Later, in AD 961 during the reign of King Edgar ('Edgar the Peaceful'), he became Archbishop of Canterbury. In this position Dunstan ruled England almost completely, for the Saxon church was more powerful than the Crown in pre-Norman times. Yet he ruled with wisdom. He introduced Benedictine codes of conduct, encouraged the arts and developed a social cohesion that bound the country together under a new enlightenment. He died in AD 988, sadly mourned across the length and breadth of his peaceful kingdom. To such a man as St Dunstan, whose interests included art and music, a crime such as the one committed in 1937 would have been incomprehensible.

To the inhabitants of Baltonsborough in the 1930s, also, the crime was beyond belief. They had known Lily Rendell all their lives, for she had been born in a neighbouring village, and had always thought her to be a kind, loving, loyal woman of great religious and moral convictions. How could anyone possibly have murdered her – and in such a violent and horrible way?

William Rendell had never been liked. He had no trade, and no regular work. He travelled about picking up jobs where he could – usually as a farm labourer. He went from village to village, town to town. Sometimes he would work away from home for months at a time, returning home only for the occasional weekend. He was restless and untrustworthy, people thought, difficult and friendless. His temper was unpredictable too. He was known to change character from morose and sullen to frantic and violent.

The couple had lived in an end-of-terrace cottage in Kite Lane, off Ham Street, at that end of Baltonsborough known as Lottisham Green. He was a good deal older than her – 70 to her 53 – but was still handsome and fit. He was about 6 ft tall, his lean frame being topped by a shock of snow-white hair. He sported grey whiskers and a beard, and held himself erect. He had served in the army when younger and still maintained a military bearing. She, on the other hand, was shorter and stouter than him. She worked as a milker, part-time, at a local farm and this had given her a permanent stoop.

Neighbours had often wondered about the Rendell marriage. 'Chalk and cheese' was the usual comment. Whilst he was shiftless and poor by nature and background, she was stable and well-off. As Lily Gertrude Stickland, she had been brought up in a property-owning family. She had inherited a number of houses and these had provided her with some regular income from rents. The house she and William lived in was hers, as were the two alongside – the Rendell cottage was the end one of a row of three.

Nevertheless, despite their differences, the two Rendells seemed to rub along well enough together. They had no children of their own but had adopted three boys. These were, in fact, nephews, sons of Lily's sister and brother-in-law, who were unable themselves to afford the upkeep of the

117

children. As they grew up and found jobs these boys left the Rendell home. At the time of the tragedy only one of them was left, the youngest.

On the morning of the 23rd April 1937, which was a Friday, the body of Lily Rendell was found in a pool of blood on the kitchen floor, at the back of her cottage. She had been battered to death. Later that day her husband was apprehended near Shepton Mallet. He admitted his guilt and was taken into custody.

On the following Wednesday, the 28th April, Lily Rendell's funeral was held at the church at nearby West Bradley. There were four pall-bearers and the coffin was made of the best elm, adorned with brass fittings. There were many friends and relatives attending, and nearly all the people of Baltonsborough village came to pay their last respects. Beautiful wreaths were laid on the grave. Lily Rendell was mourned by everyone. William Rendell – the hated, reviled William – was safely behind lock and key.

It was only later, when the full details of the tragedy became known, that people began to change their minds. And after the trial, held in the following June, more serious doubts began to arise, as to the rights and wrongs of the case and to the guilt or otherwise of William Rendell.

From the inquest (held at the Council Offices, Street, on Monday, 26th April) and from the trial (held at the Somerset Assizes, Wells, on 9th June) a clear picture can be pieced together as to the actual events that occurred on the day of the tragedy, before and after Lily Rendell's untimely death.

On the morning of Friday, 23rd April Lily went to work as usual to milk the cows at Mr Cotton's farm outside the village. She was to return home at about 8.30 am. Whilst she was out, her husband William got up and prepared breakfast and their nephew came downstairs from his room. By 9 am all three were eating breakfast.

Soon afterwards, the nephew left the house. At about 9.30 am the Rendells were seen in their little garden and both appeared happy. Mr Reginald Dowding, a smallholder of Marshes Farm in Baltonsborough, passed by at that time and all seemed well. Later that morning, however, a dispute is said to have arisen. Neighbours heard raised voices and an argument was evidently in progress. The two ladies living next door to the Rendells – Mrs Ellen Clara Helps and Mrs Harriett Elizabeth Higgins – heard the noises quite clearly, for the wall between the two houses was only a thin partition. Then screams rang out as the quarrel turned violent. Immediately, the two ladies, being alarmed, went to fetch help from Mr Billing who lived next door on the other side.

Mr Billing, who himself was an old-age pensioner, went to the Rendell house to see if he could do anything to stop the argument. But, as he approached, William Rendell appeared at the front door. The latter was putting on his overcoat. The two men met along the garden path. Billing asked Rendell if everything was all right. Rendell replied 'Oh yes'. Billing pressed his enquiry, asking if anything was the matter. Rendell replied 'Nothing'. At this William Rendell left, walking away from the cottage, out of the village. Billing, however, not being satisfied, continued up the garden path to investigate further. He knocked at the door and shouted out but received no answer. Curious by now, he pushed at the front door (which was still open) and entered. Inside, he found Lily Rendell lying on the kitchen floor with blood streaming from her body. The police and a doctor were called.

In due course Detective Constable Ashley arrived, together with Dr Struthers of Street. By this time Mrs Rendell was dead. Investigation revealed that her throat had been cut across so that her windpipe and jugular vein had severed. In all there were seven wounds, some of which were over 2½ inches long. Nearby lay a hatchet with blood stains on the handle and a razor with blood on the blade. Some hair was sticking to the latter. A bowl of bloodstained water stood close by.

The search was begun for William Rendell. He had been seen walking towards East Pennard, so a police car was sent to catch him up along the road to Shepton Mallet. He was thus apprehended at Pye Hill, not far from Pylle station, on the Somerset and Dorset railway. Detective Sergeant Burfitt approached and asked him his name. 'William Rendell', came the reply. The Detective Sergeant then said that the police had been to his house. In answer Rendell said, 'I know all about it. I was on my way to Shepton and going in to the station.' He was then conveyed into the police car. Inside the car Rendell was formally cautioned and told that he did not have to say anything. Despite this caution, Rendell said, 'I hit the missus over the head with a chopper and cut her throat with a razor I used to cut my corns.' Later, at Glastonbury police station, Rendell made a full statement. He was remanded for a week.

This sequence of events was accepted at face value by almost everyone and perceived justice took its course. At that stage few people questioned the ever-ready confession, or the lack of emotion shown throughout by the 'villain' Rendell. Few people questioned that there seemed to be a lack of motive and that Rendell appeared not to show any regrets. These questions were to come later.

The trial took place on Wednesday, 9th June 1937 at the Wells Assizes. William Rendell was represented by Mr Malcolm McGougan, barrister-at-law, and Mr John Maude prosecuted on behalf of the Crown. Rendell pleaded guilty and, throughout the hearing, stood erect and unmoved. The defence case argued for clemency, hoping that the background facts would persuade the jury and judge to show mercy. The prosecution case rested largely on Rendell's own statement and confession.

The statement was brief and gave the sequence of events outlined above. It touched upon the background facts, including the nature of the Rendell marriage. But it failed to indicate the depths to which the Rendells' relationship had sunk. It was to take the defence counsel and his witnesses to fill in the details. And what details! The Baltonsborough inhabitants soon realised that their impression of William and Lily had been totally misguided.

The marriage had never been a good one. The couple married in 1906 when William was 39 and Lily just 23. But within months they were living apart, Lily at her cottage at Lottisham Green and William in a workhouse. After about four or five years he returned to see if they could make a new start, but this attempt failed. The two were incompatible.

William was, in fact, a kindly, quiet man. Born in 1867 he joined the army as soon as he was old enough (in the 1880s) and remained in uniform for 12 years – until the last years of the century. Thereafter he tried to settle down in the Somerset countryside, turning his hand to farming. In due course he met Lily Stickland, a wild forceful girl. She fell for his charm, bearing and good nature, and he was flattered by the attention of a young, attractive girl. But it did not take long after the nuptials for William to realise his ghastly mistake.

She was fierce, uncouth, dirty and foul-mouthed. 'I had a dog's life at home', he said at the trial – a veritable understatement. She nagged him incessantly and never let him hold down a proper job, fearing he would gain some self-respect and independence. In the first year of marriage, one particular row caused her to smash every window in the house, such was her temper.

So unhappy was William that, in 1914, he joined the army again to fight in the Great War – despite the fact that he was, by then, about 47 years old and as such not liable for the call-up. As a result of seeing action in France he was injured by a piece of shrapnel. This remained embedded in his skull and gave him great physical pain for the rest of his life.

After the armistice – and throughout the 1920s – William lived in a succession of workhouses. For much of the time he was unemployed. When he was in work he occasionally returned to Lily at Baltonsborough, where he would do his best to help bring up her three nephews, who had moved into the married home as 'adopted sons'. From all accounts William was very fond of these boys.

But life at home was miserable. On many an occasion he would complain to neighbours that the food his wife gave him was not fit to eat and that the house was dirty. One witness at the trial, a Mrs Ivy Charlotte Walter of Glastonbury, confirmed that Lily had not been clean of habit – being dirty, foul-mouthed and hot-headed. Detective Constable Ashley, in his evidence, described the Rendell

## TRAGEDY AT BALTONSBOROUGH.

### WOMEN'S DEATH FROM THROAT WOUNDS.

### HUSBAND FOUND NEAR PYLLE.

CHARGE OF WILFUL MURDER BROUGHT

At the last house practically in Baltonsborough parish towards Lottisham, down a lane at the extreme end of Ham Street, there resided up to Friday morning last an elderly couple, William and Lily Rendall. The man was seventy years of age, a tall spare man with grey whiskers and beard. When he was working it was generally as a farm labourer, but up to about five weeks ago he was for some time an inmate of the Public Assistance Institution at Wells. Since taking his discharge from that place he does not appear to have done much work. Mrs. Rendall was employed as a milker by a farmer close at hand. On Friday morning she went to work as usual and carried out her task, returning home between 8 and 9 o'clock. William Rendall was about the place at that time, but when he was sought for afterwards he was missing. Later on in the morning Mrs. Rendall was found with severe throat wounds which resulted in her death within a very short time after the injury was inflicted. The police were communicated with—the nearest constable is several miles off—and medical aid sought, but the woman had already been dead some time when a doctor arrived from Street.

From circumstances reported to the Police Superintendent at Glastonbury a search was commenced for the husband of the woman. Enquiries showed that he was seen making his way towards East Pennard some miles off, and he was traced through the village, and ultimately found at Pye Hill on the road to Shepton Mallet, and not far from Pylle Station on the S. & D.J.R. Detective Sergt. Burfitt, of Glastonbury, arrested him, and he was brought back to Glastonbury Police Station. Here he was formally charged and conveyed to the cells.

From what one can gather of the events Wm. Rendall has recently become entitled to an old-age pension. Since leaving the Wells Institution he has been for a visit to Stourminster Newton, returning a fortnight ago. Mrs. Rendall, who had no children, adopted in turn three nephews one after the other as this earlier grew up. The third, Mr. W. Ford, was living at the cottage with his aunt and uncle. On the morning of Friday after Mrs. Rendall had gone milking for Mr. Cotton her husband got up and prepared the breakfast, and soon after Mrs. Rendall's return Mr. Ford left. Later in the morning a dispute appears to have arisen between husband and wife. Screams were heard by neighbours. Presently Mr. Billing saw Rendall leave the house. He asked if it was all right in there, and Rendall replied "Oh, yes," and went away. Mr. Billing seems not to have been satisfied. He went into the house and found Mrs. Rendall bleeding from throat wounds in the kitchen. Dr. Struthers, of Street, was called and the police notified.

### REMANDED TO HORFIELD.

Later in the day William Rendall was brought before Ald. J. Coleby Morland in the magistrates' room at the Court House and formally charged with the wilful murder of his wife, Lily Gertrude Rendall, that morning. Supt. Edwards, who was in charge of the case, called only one witness.

Detective Sergt. Burfitt, who proved detaining prisoner that morning at Pye Hill, in the parish of West Pennard, charging him with the murder of his wife and cautioning him. Prisoner made a statement to him.

On this evidence prisoner was remanded to Horfield for a week.

INQUEST OPENED AND ADJOURNED.

The inquest on the body of Lily Gertrude Rendall, aged 54 years, was opened on Monday evening at the Vestry Hall, Council Offices, Street, by Mr. Clarence L. Rutter, Coroner for the division, and formally adjourned until July 5th at 2 30 after evidence of identification had been given. A jury was sworn comprising Messrs E. Smith (foreman), J. J. Chubb, H. J. Clare, R. F. Green, W. Miller, F. J. Palmer and J. Underwood. Supt. Edwards, Inspector Bungay, Detective Sergt. Burfitt and P.C. Bagg were in attendance.

Clifford James Stickland, farm labourer, of Broadmoor, Butleigh, stated that the deceased woman was a cousin of his, and was 54 years of age. She resided at Lottisham Green, near Baltonsborough.

This was the whole of the evidence taken.

In adjourning the inquest as stated the Coroner said that probably it would not be necessary to call the jury together again.

### THE FUNERAL.

This took place at West Bradley Church on Wednesday afternoon, and was conducted by the Rev. A. F. M. Brown, Vicar of West Bradley and Lottisham. The service was semichoral, the hymns sung being "Jesu, lover of my soul" and "Rock of Ages cleft for me." Mrs J. Pearce was at the organ. The coffin, of polished elm with brass fittings, bore the inscription: "Lily Rendall, died April 23rd, 1937, aged 53 years." The relatives and friends

*Contemporary press coverage from the* Central Somerset Gazette *of April 30th, 1937.*

122

home as he had seen it on the morning of the tragedy. He said that it was more like a sty, being filthy and smelly. He was amazed that food could have been prepared under such conditions – it must have been unfit to eat. The bread and butter on the table was dirty; the stale meat in the cupboard looked as though it had been hanging about for some days.

Whenever William came home, from an absence of perhaps weeks or months, Lily would nag him to return to the workhouse. If he did not go back, she said, she would get the police to throw him out. But he was always loath to leave, feeling morally bound to try to make the marriage work. And, besides, he loved his little garden, which he tended with patience and care.

When William was approaching the age of 70 and was spending one of his enforced periods in a workhouse, he received a letter from Lily. She wanted to see him. Since he was shortly to be receiving his old-age pension, she said, he ought to return home in order to 'get it through'. Evidently she did not want to miss out on any extra cash. William duly obliged and returned to Baltonsborough.

But life was no better. What made matters even worse by this time was that Lily's 'friendships' were becoming less secret. He had long suspected that, in his absence, certain men became regular visitors to the Kite Lane cottage. Now Lily positively taunted him about these men. She would tell him that she could have men round her whenever she wanted them to come. On one particular weekend no fewer than three men had paid extensive visits to the house. 'What sort of house was Lily keeping?' William asked himself.

The case put forward by the defence counsel was clearly overwhelming. William – at the end of his tether – had been goaded by his wife once too often. At last, driven into a violent rage, he had turned against her. The murder may have been deliberate, but it could have been accidental, in the sense that William had struck Lily too hard during an uncontrollable fit of passion. Perhaps manslaughter might have been a more just verdict. The jury clearly thought so. It returned with a judgement of guilty but strongly recommended that mercy should be shown. The judge, however, thought otherwise and passed sentence accordingly.

But the story did not end there. One or two strands of the case remained untied. A few questions remained unanswered. Doubts persisted about William Rendell's guilt.

The court had been told there had been insanity in Lily Rendell's family. The Sticklands had not been stable and madness was a strong gene in their background. The three nephews – sons of Lily's sister – were thought to be wayward. Curiously, none of these nephews was ever called as a witness, even the youngest who was living with the Rendells at the time of the tragedy. Did William Rendell forbid his defence counsel from calling them to the witness stand? It was said that the youngest nephew had left the house before the murder was committed but no one, it seems, actually saw him leave.

William Rendell was an old, unhappy and disillusioned man who had little to live for. He had an affection for the nephews, who he thought of as sons. Did he sacrifice his own life to protect that of someone he really did love?

# INDEX

125